THE FRUIT OF THE SPIRIT

IT'S WHAT YOU ARE THAT COUNTS

Richard W. O'Ffill

Pacific Press® Publishing Association
Nampa, Idaho
Oshawa, Ontario, Canada
www.pacificpress.com

Cover design by Gerald Lee Monks
Cover design resources from Lars Justinen
Inside design by Aaron Troia

Copyright © 2009 by Pacific Press® Publishing Association
Printed in the United States of America
All rights reserved

Unless otherwise noted, Scripture quotations are from the NKJV, The New King James Version, copyright © 1979, 1980, 1982, Thomas Nelson, Inc., Publishers.

Scriptures quoted from Moffatt are from *The Bible: A New Translation,* by James Moffatt, copyright by James Moffatt 1954. Used by permission of Harper & Row, Publishers, Incorporated.

Scriptures quoted from NEB are from *The New English Bible,* copyright © The Delegates of the Oxford University Press and the Syndics of the Cambridge University Press 1961, 1970. Reprinted by permission.

The author assumes full responsibility of the accuracy of all facts and quotations as cited in this book.

You can obtain additional copies of this book by calling toll-free 1-800-765-6955 or by visiting www.adventistbookcenter.com.

Library of Congress Cataloging-in-Publication Data:

O'Ffill, Richard, 1940-
  The fruit of the spirit : it's what you are that counts / Richard W. O'Ffill.
    p. cm.
  ISBN 13: 978-0-8163-2362-3 (paperback)
  ISBN 10: 0-8163-2362-3 (paperback)
  1. Fruit of the Spirit. I. Title.
  BV4501.3.O385   2009
  234'.13—dc22

                                                2009023775

09 10 11 12 13 • 5 4 3 2 1

TABLE OF CONTENTS

CHAPTER 1

IT'S WHAT YOU ARE THAT COUNTS

"I will give you a new heart and put a new spirit within you; . . . I will put My Spirit within you and cause you to walk in My statutes, and you will keep My judgments and do them."

—*Ezekiel 36:26, 27*

It was Sabbath morning, and I was a visitor. The Sabbath School teacher was talking about the Holy Spirit. She said, "Let's pray that the Holy Spirit will be poured out."

With a smile, I raised my hand. "He's already being poured out," I offered. "Let's pray that we will receive Him!"

In recent years, the ministry of the Holy Spirit seems to have become the patrimony of the charismatics, who have taken it upon themselves to be the ones to decide who has the Holy Spirit and who doesn't. To them, it's all about the *gifts* of the Spirit. They have prioritized the gifts, and if a person doesn't have the gift they deem most important, then they declare that person doesn't have the Holy Spirit at all. I like what my dad used to say: we shouldn't talk about the gifts of the Spirit until we talk about the fruit of the Spirit.

Many—myself included—are longing for the Savior to come and are anxious to do anything that will hasten His coming. Yet there's a danger that what is intended to be a means to an end becomes an end in itself. More than that, it can become a litmus test distinguishing between those who have arrived in the Christian life and those who haven't.

I often hear people express the conviction that we ought to be healing the sick, casting out devils, and doing other supernatural acts that were performed by members of the early church. I've noticed that some who want to perform miracles basically want to get power. Power is a good thing, but it belongs to God and not to us. We can desire it and pray for it, but we cannot demand it when and where we want it. God decides the time and the place. Jesus promised, " 'You shall receive power when the Holy Spirit has come upon you; and you shall be witnesses to Me in Jerusalem, and in all Judea and Samaria, and to the end of the earth' "(Acts 1:8). Evidence indicates that the Holy Spirit is already being poured out. And we are told that God's giving will crescendo as we approach the close of probation.

Jesus confronted those who wanted to see signs and wonders as a condition for believing in Him. When some of the scribes and Pharisees asked Him for a sign, He answered, " 'An evil and adulterous generation seeks after a sign, and no sign will be given to it except the sign of the prophet Jonah' " (Matthew 12:39). Jesus taught that there is something more meaningful than miracles, something more superb than the spectacular.

I am the son of an Adventist minister. I remember what it meant to be a Seventh-day Adventist when I was a child. Being an Adventist then was a lifestyle. We were thought of as a people who didn't smoke, didn't drink, didn't wear jewelry, didn't go to movies or dances, and who kept Saturday as the Sabbath. And keeping the Sabbath meant we didn't listen to the radio, didn't watch television, didn't read newspapers, didn't go to work, and didn't buy or sell.

Dad wouldn't let us read the comics, we couldn't listen to jazz or murder programs on the radio, and we were serious about health. We didn't smoke or drink alcoholic beverages. Coffee, tea, and Coca-Cola were not allowed. We didn't use mustard, vinegar, or black pepper. Of course, we ate no meat.

I had the good fortune of attending church school, academy, and college. In those days, a student could be expelled or suspended for going to movies, holding hands with a date, not honoring the dress codes, and, of course, for smoking or drinking. In other words, if you had asked me back then what it meant to be a Seventh-day Adventist, I would have given you a long list of the things we didn't do, because that was pretty much the way we saw it.

Having said this, I would like to state that I have no regrets about living that lifestyle. I don't think we were wrong when we taught that we shouldn't eat pork. But looking back, I see we should have emphasized being kind.

We weren't wrong in preaching that the Sabbath is the seventh-day of the week and that God expects us to honor Him by keeping it holy. But we should have also emphasized not being mean.

No, we weren't wrong—narrow and shallow maybe, but not wrong.

BELIEVING, DOING, AND BEING

When one became a member of the church then—and often now as well—it seems to have been taken for granted that one had been born again. In the good old days, a person could be an Adventist in good and regular standing and not be born again. Adventism was about believing and doing; not much emphasis was given to being. All you had to do was to conform to the rules. Baptist parents will say how happy they are that last Sunday Johnny "got saved." Adventist parents usually say how happy they are that last Sabbath Jennifer was baptized.

When the essence of the Christian life is perceived to consist in not doing things, we're in trouble. While getting victory over sin is foundational to a life in Christ, it's critical that there be even more. Jesus cautioned,

"When an unclean spirit goes out of a man [the man is baptized], he goes through dry places, seeking rest, and finds none. Then he says, 'I will return to my house from which I came.' And when he comes, he finds it empty, swept, and put in order. [The man's life is clean outwardly but not filled with the things of God.] Then he goes and takes with him seven other spirits more wicked than himself, and they enter and dwell there; and the last state of that man is worse than the first" (Matthew 12:43–45).

Although the first work of the gospel in the life must be a cleansing from sin, this work is only a preparation for what comes next, and that is the infilling of the Holy Spirit. " 'I will give you a new heart and put a new spirit within you; I will take the heart of stone out of your flesh and give you a heart of flesh [the new birth]. I will put My Spirit within you' " (Ezekiel 36:26, 27).

The promise in these verses has two components. The first is that God will give us a new spirit—that is, a new us. As Jesus explained to Nicodemus, we must be born again (John 3:3). The rest of the promise states that when we've been born again, God will put His Spirit within us, to dwell in the new us. The apostle Paul wrote, "If anyone is in Christ, he *is* a new creation; old things have passed away; behold, all things have become new" (2 Corinthians 5:17; emphasis added).

If God is to dwell with us, He must have a habitation. Before He could breathe the spirit of life into Adam, He had to create a body to hold it. Israel had to build the tabernacle and later the temple before God could come down and dwell with them. Similarly, God created human hearts for His dwelling. He has given us new hearts and put a new spirit within us as the indispensable condition of His dwelling in us.

Sadly, God's original plan for humanity was frustrated. Jesus' life, death, and resurrection were meant not only to break the power of sin but to re-create a dwelling place of which it could be said, " 'The kingdom of God is within you' " (Luke 17:21).

When Jesus walked this earth as a man, He was personally with His disciples. However, it was not until Pentecost that the promise of John 14:16, 17 was fulfilled: " 'I will pray the Father, and He will give you another Helper, that He may abide with you forever—the Spirit of truth, whom the world cannot receive, because it neither sees Him nor knows Him; but you know Him, for He dwells with you and will be in you.' " Another wonderful and sobering thought is expressed in 1 Corinthians 6:19, 20: "Do you not know that your body is the temple of the Holy Spirit who is in you, whom you have from God, and you are not your own? For you were bought at a price; therefore glorify God in your body and in your spirit, which are God's."

While abstaining from smoking and drinking and going to movies and dancing, and omitting mustard, vinegar, and black pepper from one's diet, and worshiping on the seventh day, and following a dress code are laudable, none of these things requires that one be born again—or, for that matter, even that one be a follower of Christ. Most Hare Krishnas are vegans. A true Christian is one whose heart is not only swept and clean but is filled in a wonderful and mysterious way with the Holy Spirit. If and when we can comprehend this truth, the effect on our personal lives, our families, and, subsequently, on the life of the church, will be immediate.

As we welcome the Holy Spirit and He begins His work, spiritual fruit will begin to grow in our lives, producing, in essence, the very character of our Lord and Savior Jesus Christ. We are well acquainted with the spiritual qualities listed in Galatians 5:22, 23: "The fruit of the Spirit is love, joy, peace, longsuffering, kindness, goodness, faithfulness, gentleness, self-control." This list, however, is not exhaustive. There are other spiritual qualities as well, such as those enumerated in 1 Timothy 6:11, Romans 5:3–5, 2 Timothy 3:10, and 2 Peter 1:5–7.

THE DECIDING FACTOR

Those who claim to be followers of Jesus but who do not produce this fruit will be plucked up and taken away (John 15:2). Jesus also declared that because many will profess to be His followers (Matthew 7:21, 22), the deciding factor will not be what they profess to believe or even the works they do, but rather the kind of people they are (Mathew 12:33).

For example, a text generally used as a guideline for how women should dress contains much more than a dress code. It assures us that the Christian life doesn't begin on the outside but rather on the inside: "Do not let your adornment be merely outward—arranging the hair, wearing gold, or putting on fine apparel—rather let it be the hidden person of the heart, with the incorruptible beauty of a gentle and quiet spirit, which is very precious in the sight of God" (1 Peter 3:3, 4).

Considering our emphases as Seventh-day Adventists in days gone by, Jesus might say to us, "These things ought you to have done, but not left the other undone." Our lifestyle did not so much require a change of heart as a change of mind. The indwelling of the Holy Spirit doesn't lessen the impact of the letter of the law in our lives, but it will assure that we have the spirit of the law. While people can keep the letter of the law without the indwelling of the Holy Spirit, those who truly have the Spirit in their hearts will not only keep the letter of the law but the spirit of the law as well.

To some extent, we may be reaping the backlash from a superficial gospel that appears to change the outside but leaves the heart vulnerable to being occupied by attitudes that, as in the case of the Pharisees, can make our message a heavy yoke and expose a certain hypocrisy.

It will be those who not only have been "swept" and "cleaned" but who also have become the dwelling place of the Holy Spirit and, as a result, have manifested His fruit in their lives who will receive the seal of God. While we pray for the outpouring of the latter rain, we must be aware that this gift will be given for a special purpose—it will be given to prepare a living people to meet a living Lord. And it will be given only to those whose lives exhibit love, joy, peace, patience, kindness, goodness, faithfulness, gentleness, and self-control. This realization should inspire us to contemplate and pray for the fruit of the Spirit.

The True Vine

I have noticed that when some people get around the table and begin to discuss spiritual things, they talk about an arm's-length gospel, or perhaps how to live a Christian life by the numbers. There are often heated discussions about the nature of Christ, the health message, the meaning of grace, or how to meet felt needs; yet there is usually little reference to the fruit of the Spirit and what the fruit means in the life of a born-again Christian. The fruit of the Spirit is not Heaven's wish list for the believer. Rather, it is what is given to a person who abides in the Vine, and it will be the deciding factor for those who will finally be saved. Jesus left little room for discussion when He declared:

> "I am the true vine, and My Father is the vinedresser. Every branch in Me that does not bear fruit He takes away; and every branch that bears fruit He prunes, that it may bear more fruit. You are already clean because of the word which I have spoken to you. Abide in Me, and I in you. As the branch cannot bear

fruit of itself, unless it abides in the vine, neither can you, unless you abide in Me. I am the vine, you are the branches. He who abides in Me, and I in him, bears much fruit; for without Me you can do nothing. If anyone does not abide in Me, he is cast out as a branch and is withered; and they gather them and throw them into the fire, and they are burned" (John 15:1–6).

A potato chip commercial famous in the past challenged, "Bet you can't eat just one." So it is with the fruit of the Spirit. A person can't have just one. It will help us to think of these spiritual qualities as petals on a flower. Although the blooming of the flower is a process, the petals unfold together. We may not come to maturity in these qualities all at once, but they will develop in tandem with each other. For example, a kind person will not be impatient or proud.

You probably have noticed the many ads for products that claim to do away with wrinkles, develop abs, or otherwise make a person look at least ten years younger. The magic may come in a lotion or as an exercise machine. Buy it, use it, and—*voilà*—you have it. However, we don't need Botox but something much better—a new heart. The Christian life is more than meets the eye.

When I was a student at Washington Missionary College (now Washington Adventist University), I took a class in natural history. The course required us to be able to identify a tree branch without its leaves. I'm sorry to say (and my grade in the class reflected it) I never caught on. But I wouldn't have had any problem if I could have seen the leaf or the fruit. While the Christian life is about *doing* (bearing fruit), this doing will be hollow and meaningless unless it is driven by *being*. And this means being transformed by the indwelling Spirit of God, whose first work is to convict us of sin, who then gives us ongoing victory over sin, and finally, who fills us with the most wonderful gift of all, the fruit of the Spirit—which, in a word, is the mind of Christ.

When we see God's plan for our lives, we might at first be thrilled and challenged, but later feel overwhelmed. Not to worry. The promise is that He who has begun this good work—fruit-bearing—in us has promised to complete it (Philippians 1:6). The Holy Spirit doesn't do things halfway!

At the end of all but the last of the following chapters, there will be an assignment entitled "Thinking It Over." This is meant not only to stimulate your thinking, but also to challenge you to envision what will develop as you cultivate the fruit of the Spirit in your life wherever you happen to be in the process.

As you read this book, please resist the thought that everyone needs this but you. Think of the needs of your own heart. This point is expressed by the words of the old song "Not my brother, not my sister, but it's me, O Lord, standing in the need of prayer." The fruit of the Spirit must manifest itself in the church on a one-by-one basis. And you must be that one.

CHAPTER 2

I'M SUPPOSED TO LOVE WHO?

> *If your enemy is hungry,*
> > *give him bread to eat;*
> *And if he is thirsty,*
> > *give him water to drink;*
> *For so you will heap coals of fire*
> > *on his head,*
> *And the LORD will reward you.*
> > —*Proverbs 25:21, 22*

When it comes time to decorate for Christmas, I usually end up having to buy a few strings of lights for our tree. The lights make the tree. In fact, back in the early mists of time, Christmas tree decorations were usually candles and nothing more. Over the years, Christmas tree decorations have evolved until now artificial trees come with their own built-in lights. But every now and then, I need a string or two of separate minilights, so off I go to Home Depot.

The lights come in boxes—cords neatly wound on a plastic frame or bundled with rubber bands. I unwind them and put them on the tree.

But when the time comes to take the tree down and put the lights away, more often than not, I just stuff them into boxes or plastic bags. It shouldn't be a surprise, then, that the next year when I'm ready to put the lights on the tree again, they're all tangled up. It takes time and patience to untangle the cords, especially when I have more important things to do.

In the list of the qualities that make up the fruit of the Spirit, love is mentioned first. It's the hook from which all the other fruit hang. But *love* is a word that has become all tangled up, like Christmas tree lights, and unless we can untangle it, we'll never understand its true meaning. Misunderstanding, in turn, prevents us from appreciating the depths of what Jesus meant when He said, " 'God so loved the world that He gave His only begotten Son' " (John 3:16). Nor will we understand how we can love God with all our hearts and our neighbors as ourselves.

As you know, the devil hates God and everything about Him, especially the fact that God is love; so he does all he can to cheapen the concept of love and render it worthless. Consequently, the word *love* is not only overused, but very often wrongly used. It may come as a shock to the person in the street, but love isn't sex. Neither is it how we feel about apple pie, a new suit, a trip to the Bahamas, or the car we just bought. It would serve us well to find other words to express these other meanings. Someone who says she loves the color blue really means she prefers that color. A preference is not love, and to use the word in this way devalues it.

Just caring about someone isn't love either. One can care to the point of obsession or lust.

One of the characteristics of the people who live in the last days is that they love themselves—that is, they put themselves and their needs before anyone else. Because of this, the Bible declares that the world will become unsafe: "Know this, that in the last days perilous times will come: for men will be lovers of themselves" (2 Timothy 3:1, 2).

Some have the temerity to allege that many of the social problems afflicting us arise because we don't love ourselves. However, according to 2 Timothy 3:1, 2, this can't be true. We must also take into consideration Ephesians 5:29. It says, "No one ever hated his own flesh, but nourishes and cherishes it, just as the Lord does the church."

Out of curiosity, I once skimmed through a book that encourages people to love themselves. It gave one particularly fascinating illustration of how to accomplish this. The author suggested, in complete seriousness, that a man take his wife to a cozy restaurant, the kind with candlelight and soft music. To my mind, this would be a nice Italian restaurant. Next, at just the right time, the husband should look at his wife tenderly and whisper, "I love me."

If this suggestion weren't so pathetic, it would be amusing. Humankind has always been selfish, but we knew that orientation wasn't right. These days selfishness is actually encouraged! How can a couple stay married when the spouses love themselves best?

What is being passed off as love in the world today is the opposite of what the gospel is all about. Jesus said we are to love each other, to deny ourselves, and to not think more highly of ourselves than we ought. The world today is saying just the opposite.

WHAT LOVE IS

First Corinthians 13 tells us what love is and what it is not. The apostle Paul begins this chapter by showing the primacy of love: "Though I speak with the tongues of men and of angels, but have not love [that is, love as revealed in Jesus], I have become sounding brass or a clanging cymbal. And though I have the gift of prophecy, and understand all mysteries and all knowledge, and though I have all faith, so that I could remove mountains, but have not love, I am nothing" (verses 1, 2).

Continuing—using everyday language: Even if I cash in everything I own to feed the poor (verse 3), it's a meaningless donation unless I do it with true love. Next Paul says the same thing about martyrdom. The point is that a person can do all the right things—good things, generous things—but for the wrong reasons.

What are some of the wrong reasons for doing good deeds? To be noticed and admired, to impress people, to make ourselves appear as saints, to get a front-row seat in heaven, because someone told us to, etc. There are lots of poor reasons for doing good, but the only legitimate reason in the books of heaven is to do it out of love.

So, what *is* love? What's it all about? How does it work?

The next part of 1 Corinthians 13 expresses what we might call the anatomy of love. True love is patient, kind, and unselfish. It isn't proud or envious.

Pride is the mother of all sins, and its progeny is selfishness. Incredibly, pride and selfishness were born in the heart of the archangel Lucifer, who stood in the very presence of God. This is so inconceivable it's called the mystery of iniquity. Of him Scripture says,

> "How you are fallen from heaven,
> O Lucifer, son of the morning!
> How you are cut down to the ground,
> You who weakened the nations!
> For you have said in your heart:
> 'I will ascend into heaven,
> I will exalt my throne above the stars of God;
> I will also sit on the mount of the congregation
> On the farthest sides of the north;
> I will ascend above the heights of the clouds,
> I will be like the Most High' " (Isaiah 14:12–14).

Love and pride cannot and will not coexist. The Bible clearly describes the ultimate result of pride:

- "You rebuke the proud—the cursed, / Who stray from Your commandments" (Psalm 119:21).
- "Everyone proud in heart is an abomination to the LORD; / Though they join forces, none will go unpunished" (Proverbs 16:5).
- " 'Behold, the day is coming, burning like an oven, and all the proud, yes, all who do wickedly will be stubble. And the day which is coming shall burn them up,' says the LORD of hosts, 'that will leave them neither root nor branch' " (Malachi 4:1).
- "You younger people, submit yourselves to your elders. Yes, all of you be submissive to one another, and be clothed with humility, for 'God resists the proud, but gives grace to the humble' " (1 Peter 5:5).

There's a sharp contrast between God's love and the world's love. It reminds me of the tourist who was visiting New York City. He was walking down the sidewalk and had somehow lost his way. So he stopped a local and asked for directions. The New Yorker seemed anxious to help. "You see that traffic light? Go there and turn left. No, don't do that. Go down about three blocks and take a right. No, that's not the way. Go back to the second traffic light and . . . Come to think of it, you can't get there from here." That's the way it is when we try to mix the contemporary thinking about love and what the Bible teaches is true love. You can't get there from here!

THE TROUBLE WITH COMMERCIALS

True love doesn't envy. Envy is a spin-off of pride and selfishness. Have you considered all the many ways society encourages and nurtures envy? One of those ways is through advertisements and commercials. Madison Avenue has discovered that in order to entice a person to buy a particular product, the advertising for that product must create envy and greed. A whole new vocabulary has been developed for this purpose—such as "gotta have." Most commercials use beautiful women and handsome men to promote their products. And this is called "sexy," another advertising word.

These days a person doesn't have to look out the window and envy his next door neighbor's new car for very long. A bank loan or a credit card will even the score instantly. We thought that slavery was a thing of the past, but how many of us are owned by a little piece of plastic? Maybe we need to hear more sermons on the tenth commandment— "Thou shalt not covet"—or envy!

The kingdom of Satan has an evil trinity—pride, selfishness, and envy. These were the very first sins. They began in Satan's heart, infected our first parents, and spread to the entire human race. You and I were born with the disease. That's why we must be born again—this time into the kingdom of heaven, which is about loving God and each other. " 'A new commandment I give to you, that you love one another; as I have loved you, that you also love one another. By this all will know that you are My disciples, if you have love for one another' " (John 13:34, 35).

Through the years, I've learned that if I love God, I'll love people; and if I don't love people, I won't love God. After fifty years of marriage, I know a few things I didn't know before. One of them is that when things are not right between Betty and me, it immediately affects my relationship with God. That's why John, the apostle of love, wrote, "Beloved, let us love one another, for love is of God; and everyone who loves is born of God and knows God. He who does not love does not know God, for God is love. . . . Beloved, if God so loved us, we also ought to love one another" (1 John 4:7–11).

God wants to use the closeness of the family tie to teach us about His love. And then He wants to stretch and enlarge that tie to include all of His children. One Sabbath as I was sitting on the platform before the sermon and looking out over the congregation, I was reminded that the church is the sum of the families that comprise it. I wonder, how are we as a church family—sons and daughters of God—demonstrating God's love? Are our homes little heavens on earth? Does our faithfulness to each other demonstrate our faithfulness to God? How we answer these questions is critical because "if someone says, 'I love God,' and hates his brother, he is a liar; for he who does not love his brother whom he has seen, how can he love God whom he has not seen? And this commandment we have from Him: that he who loves God must love his brother also" (1 John 4:20, 21).

One of my dear mother-in-law's favorite songs was "Family of God." The words of this song by Bill and Gloria Gaither are a description of the church that has the fruit of love:

> You will notice we say "brother and sister" 'round here,
> It's because we're a family and these are so near;
> When one has a heartache we all share the tears,
> And rejoice in each victory in this family so dear.[1]

Unfortunately, some churches I have visited were anything but families of God. This happens when members try to separate their relationship with God from their relationship with each other. According to Scripture, this can't be done.

So serious is the matter of not getting along in church that in the Sermon on the Mount, Jesus told His listeners that if they were on their way to church on Sabbath morning and remembered they needed to apologize to someone in the church, they should go home and not come to church until they had made it right with that person (Matthew 5:23, 24). I have often wondered how many people would be in church if we actually implemented this counsel. Unfortunately, our disagreements are usually over ridiculous things, like the two church board members who got into a shouting match over who was responsible for buying the toilet paper for the restrooms!

In the church of God today brotherly love is greatly lacking. Many of those who profess to love the Saviour neglect to love those who are united with them in Christian fellowship. We are of the same faith, members of one family, all children of the same heavenly Father, with the same blessed hope of immortality. How close and tender should be the tie that binds us together! The people of the world are watching us, to see if our faith is exerting a sanctifying influence upon our hearts. They are quick to discern every defect in our lives, every inconsistency in our actions. Let us give them no occasion to reproach our faith.[2]

FROM THE DIFFICULT TO THE IMPOSSIBLE

We have touched on having love for our home family and our church family. We admit we need to work on these areas, as difficult as it may be. Now we go from the difficult to the impossible—dealing with our enemies. That's another matter altogether. Surely we don't have to have any relationship with our enemies! Enemies are . . . well, enemies. They're to be despised and hated.

But Jesus came along and preached about loving our enemies. This is too much. Nevertheless, it's exactly what He did. His command? "Turn the other cheek."

When someone I know learned what the Bible said about turning the other cheek, he told me that, sure, he would turn the other cheek all right—and then he would "knock the guy's head off"! Would you agree that this is not what our Lord had in mind?

Now pay close attention, because perhaps the greatest test of true love is what Jesus said as recorded in Luke 6:27–35:

"I say to you who hear: Love your enemies, do good to those who hate you, bless those who curse you, and pray for those who spitefully use you. To him who strikes you on the one cheek, offer the other also. And from him who takes away your cloak, do not withhold your tunic either. Give to everyone who asks of you. And from him who takes away your goods do not ask them back. And just as you want men to do to you, you also do to them likewise. But if you love those who love you, what credit is that to you? For even sinners love those who love them. And if you do good to those who do good to you, what credit is that to you? For even sinners do the same. And if you lend to those from whom you hope to receive back, what credit is that to you? For even sinners lend to sinners to receive as much back. But love your enemies, do good, and lend, hoping for nothing in return; and your reward will be great, and you will be sons of the Most High. For He is kind to the unthankful and evil."

We often read these verses as the Scripture reading at a worship service or in our private devotions. But do we take them seriously, or do we consider them impossible to put into practice? When we're discussing the time of trouble and the persecution that will be leveled against the people of God, some people point out the necessity of victory over every sin and besetment and of reflecting the image of Christ fully. This is all well and good. But why do we fear only the sin of receiving the mark of the beast or of apostatizing or of falling for Satan's impersonation of Christ, and at the same time downplay the sins of backbiting, pride, gossip, and criticism? Are some sins worse than others?

Give your enemy what he needs without having any expectations, Jesus said. Treat your enemy kindly. The golden rule is not so much about treating our friends as we want them to treat us but about treating our enemies as we would want to be treated.

Back to our definition of love. True love isn't rude. It doesn't have a temper and plot to do others harm. True love doesn't get a kick out of hearing that someone has run off with someone else's spouse. True love does what it can to ease the burdens of others. It is optimistic and patient. True love isn't here today and gone tomorrow.

No, love isn't sex. Neither is it how we may feel about apple pie, a new suit, a trip to the Bahamas, or the car we just bought. Love is what Jesus shows for us and what we must, in turn, reflect in our relationships with others, especially our enemies—be they in the family, at church, or wherever. This kind of love comes only as a gift of the Holy Spirit and is at the heart of the theme of this book about the fruit of the Spirit. As we study the fruit of the Spirit, we will understand that it's what we are that truly matters.

---

1. Copyright © 1970, William J. Gaither, Inc.
2. Ellen G. White, "One With Christ in God," *The Southern Watchman,* February 2, 1904.

THINKING IT OVER
1. Identify one area in your life in which your love for your family, as measured by 1 Corinthians 13, is falling short.
2. Choose two elements of love that you want to upgrade in your life with God's help. Plan specifically how and when you will do this.
3. To whom do you have the most difficulty relating? In what specific ways can you manifest to that person the love Jesus has for you?

CHAPTER 3

DOWN, BUT NOT OUT

These things write we to you, that your joy may be full.

—1 John 1:4

If you were asked to define the word *joy,* how would you answer? Might you respond with the word *happiness?*

One Sabbath I decided to ask those who came to Sabbath School to fill out a little questionnaire I had prepared. There were only two questions. The first was, "What do you think is the meaning of the word *joy?*" And the second question was, "What do you think is the meaning of the word *happiness?*"

The responses to the question about the meaning of the word *joy* were particularly interesting. Among them were "a bubbly feeling," "a warm fuzzy feeling," "a feeling of happiness," and "to be happy."

When I reviewed the answers, two things became evident: People use the word *happy* more frequently than the word *joy.* And they think joy and happiness are pretty much the same thing.

But when I went to the Word of God, I discovered that the word *happiness* appears twenty-five times in it—nineteen times in the Old

Testament and six times in the New Testament—while the word *joy* is used 155 times—96 times in the Old Testament and 59 in the New. Furthermore, it became evident that these words have different meanings. A close look at the context in which these words were used reveals that happiness comes about because of something that has occurred—such as a victory over enemies or a good harvest. On the other hand, joy happens in spite of something—such as hardship or persecution.

Happiness, then, depends on circumstances, but joy is independent of all circumstances and situations. Do you see the difference?

Suppose (and I wish it were so) that Betty and I are planning a trip to the Butchart Gardens near Victoria, British Columbia—as near to heaven as you can get on this earth. We have our tickets and are making the final arrangements when something unforeseen comes along, and we have to cancel the trip. Would I be unhappy that we had to miss the trip? Yes. Would it affect my joy? No. We would have been happy to go, but our lives are so full of other delightful blessings that we would still have joy in spite of having to cancel the trip.

I like the way a friend of mine expressed it. She said that happiness is to joy what weather is to climate. Happiness is transient; oftentimes it comes or goes, depending on the circumstances. Happiness is a feeling that people pursue and can capture in short bursts. On the other hand, joy is a deeper, longer-lasting state of mind. Joy doesn't depend on circumstances. Joy is sustained and stable. Joy can endure suffering and difficult times, whereas happiness often evaporates quickly.

I think she hit it pretty close.

We can buy happiness, but we can't buy joy. Joy is where we find it. As someone explained, "Two men look out through the same bars: One sees the mud, and one the stars."[1] Joy looks beyond today. Of course, it includes today, but it's more. It's a perspective that isn't short term but one that sees tomorrow's possibilities.

There are two qualities that "enable" joy—that is, they make it work. One is faith, and the other is hope. Faith and hope are, as it were, the legs that hold joy up and make it dynamic—something that is alive and well in all circumstances. Which of the two comes first—faith or hope? Please don't stay up all night debating this; it seems to me that hope comes first. I believe hope precedes faith because Hebrews 11:1 says, "Faith is the substance of *things hoped for,* the evidence of things not seen" (emphasis added). Moffatt puts it, "Faith means that we are confident of what we hope for." The New English Bible says, "Faith gives substance to our hopes." So I conclude that faith sustains our hope, and hope gives us joy.

I once heard someone say, with tongue in cheek, "I feel so much better now that I've given up hope." Of course, this is ridiculous. When we lose hope, joy evaporates. The prophet said it right: "Although the fig tree shall not blossom, neither shall fruit be in the vines; the labour of the olive shall fail, and the fields shall yield no meat; the flock shall be cut off from the fold, and there shall be no herd in the stalls: Yet I will rejoice in the LORD, I will joy in the God of my salvation" (Habakkuk 3:17, 18, KJV). This is an excellent verse to memorize and repeat in these difficult financial times.

Like all the other fruit of the Spirit, joy shines best in the worst of times. I was in a jewelry store buying a new battery for my watch, and I couldn't help but notice the beautiful diamonds and other precious stones on display. What accentuated their beauty and sparkle was the special light that was shining directly on them, in contrast to the darkened background.

PAUL'S JOY

On our way home from a term of mission service in Pakistan, Betty and I took advantage of the opportunity to visit Europe. Along the way, we went to Rome. The apostle Paul spent the last years of his life in that ancient city. Tradition holds that in the time before his execution, he languished in the Mamertine Prison, which is located on the east side of Capitoline Hill.

The Mamertine Prison consists of two gloomy underground cells. The upper room of the prison is trapezoidal in shape. It dates from the second century B.C. The lower room is called the Tullianum. Condemned prisoners spent their last days in this room.

As we looked through the dark hole into the miserable lower room where Paul, who was perhaps the greatest preacher of all time, may have lived for two years before his execution, it was as if we could hear his words of faith and hope that led to his joy: "We are troubled on every side, yet not distressed; we are perplexed, but not in despair; persecuted, but not forsaken; cast down, but not destroyed" (2 Corinthians 4:8, 9, KJV). "I have fought a good fight, I have finished my course, I have kept the faith: henceforth there is laid up for me a crown of righteousness, which the Lord, the righteous judge, shall give me at that day: and not to me only, but unto all them also that love his appearing" (2 Timothy 4:7, 8, KJV).

The most heinous crime ever committed was the murder of the Son of God. There is a word for it—*deicide*. Death by crucifixion had no symbolic significance; its purpose was to make the death of the condemned slow, painful, and public. Nails were driven through the wrists of the criminals, not the palms because nail-pierced palms couldn't support the weight of the body. The majority of those crucified died of dehydration and fatigue, not of blood loss or the injuries. The crucified might live for days before they finally died. Sometimes their legs were broken to hasten their death.

In ancient Roman times, anyone who had a cross loaded on his shoulders and who was marched down the road toward the place of crucifixion had better have already said Goodbye to his friends. He wouldn't be coming back. The cross made no compromises. It moderated nothing, and it left nothing. When the cross struck, it struck hard and cruelly, and when it had finished its work, its victim was dead.

People didn't "do time" on the cross as they might in prison.

Yet Jesus, "for the *joy* that was set before him endured the cross, despising the shame, and is set down at the right hand of the throne of God. For consider him that endured such contradiction of sinners against himself, lest ye be wearied and faint in your minds" (Hebrews 12:2, 3, KJV; emphasis added).

Recent archaeological discoveries have uncovered letters written by martyrs during the trying centuries that followed the ascension of Christ. Just before his death, one saint penned these words: "In a dark hole I have found cheerfulness; in a place of bitterness I have found laughter, where others fear, I have found strength. Who would believe that in a state of misery I have great pleasure; that in a lonely corner I have had glorious company, and in the hardest bonds perfect repose. All of these things Jesus has granted me. He is with me, comforts me, and fills me with joy. He drives bitterness from me and fills me with strength and consolation."[2]

What does this say to you and to me? The truth is, Jesus will never leave us or forsake us (Hebrews 13:5). Notice what the apostle James wrote: "My brethren, count it all *joy* when you fall into various trials, knowing that the testing of your faith produces patience. But let patience have its perfect work, that you may be perfect and complete, lacking nothing" (James 1:2–4; emphasis added).

And from Peter, who tradition holds was crucified upside down: "In this you greatly rejoice, though now for a little while, if need be, you have been grieved by various trials, that the genuineness of your faith, being much more precious than gold that perishes, though it is tested by fire, may be found to praise, honor, and glory at the revelation of Jesus Christ, whom having not seen you love. Though now you do not see Him, yet believing, you rejoice with *joy* inexpressible and full of glory" (1 Peter 1:6–8; emphasis added).

Friend, it is the fruit of joy that gives meaning to the text, "We know that all things work together for good to those who love God, to those who are the called according to His purpose" (Romans 8:28).

I have a friend named Joni. She spends all her waking hours in a wheelchair. She told me she contracted a crippling form of arthritis when she was only twelve years old.

The first time I met Joni, I said to her, "You must find that wheelchair confining."

"Confining?" she replied. "Not confining; it's liberating."

I have never met a person who radiated more joy—this fruit of the Spirit. Joni's joy is not manufactured for the cameras or for interviews, which are many. It comes from the heart. After all, it's what we are at heart that counts.

JOY-STEALERS

While it would probably be safe to say that joy will drive away discouragement, pessimism, and guilt, yet these same attitudes, if allowed to take hold of us, will rob us of our joy. They are some of the sins that, as Hebrews 12:1 puts it, so easily ensnare us.

My mother-in-law lived for ninety-two years. Toward the end of her life, I received a call from my wife, urging me to go at once to the emergency room because Mom had fallen. As we waited for news about her condition, I remembered that at four o'clock that afternoon I had an appointment with the conference administration. I told Betty that I had to go but would return as soon as I could.

When I walked into the office of a conference official, he asked, "Dick, do you know what we've been doing?" Frankly, I didn't, although I had heard that due to some serious financial difficulties, the decision had been made to lay off fifty employees. The official continued, "We're eliminating your job as of December 31. You'll receive your salary until April 30."

How bad can things get? A beloved mother-in-law was dying and I had lost my job—all in the same day.

Was I happy? You've got to be kidding. I could hardly believe what was happening. Yet looking back, I can see that my hope sustained me. It gave me the joy of knowing that there would be a better day.

Mom passed away a little while later. But as a family we have joy, a joy that is based on the blessed hope—a hope, in turn, sustained by faith that one day the trumpet will sound and the dead in Christ (the members of my family, and yours as well) who have died in the blessed hope will rise first. "Then we who are alive and remain shall be caught up together with them in the clouds to meet the Lord in the air. And thus we shall always be with the Lord" (1 Thessalonians 4:17). Then Jesus will make all things new (Revelation 21:5), and He will wipe away all tears from our eyes (verse 4). There will be no more losing our jobs, falling down, or dying. Between now and then, we may not always be happy, but we can have the joy of looking for that better day.

The Bible says, "Rejoice in the Lord always. Again I will say, rejoice!" (Philippians 4:4). It would be impossible to "rejoice always" if it weren't for those other three key words: "in the Lord." We don't get all thrilled and happy because we're experiencing hardship. That attitude would be not only unrealistic, it would be unhealthy. Our encouragement, our hope, our joy, is in the Lord.

The joy that God's people experienced throughout the centuries didn't make the pain or the suffering and hardship go away. But because joy is the result of faith and hope, it gave them strength to bear whatever happened to them.

I love to sing the song that Wayne Hooper, one of the original members of The King's Heralds quartet, wrote as the theme song for the General Conference Session of 1962:

> We have this hope that burns within our hearts,
> Hope in the coming of the Lord.
> We have this faith that Christ alone imparts,

Faith in the promise of His Word.

We believe the time is here,

When the nations far and near

Shall awake, and shout, and sing

Hallelujah! Christ is King!

We have this hope that burns within our hearts,

Hope in the coming of the Lord.[3]

The words remind me of the encouragement from the servant of the Lord: "We have nothing to fear for the future, except as we shall forget the way the Lord has led us, and His teaching in our past history."[4]

---

1. Frederick Langbridge wrote these lines.

2. Charles Hembree, *Pocket of Pebbles* (Grand Rapids, Mich.: Baker Book House, 1969), 33.

3. Copyright © 1962 by Wayne Hooper.

4. Ellen G. White, *Life Sketches* (Nampa, Idaho: Pacific Press® Publishing Association, 1943), 196.

THINKING IT OVER

1. Make two lists, one of the things that make you happy and the other of the things that bring you joy. How would you react if you were to lose any or all of the items in either list? To which list do you give priority?

2. No doubt at some time you've shared with someone why you were happy about something. Now, tell a member of your family or a close friend what gives you joy. Do this today, or tomorrow at the latest.

3. Usually when we pray, we tell the Lord our troubles and ask Him for blessings. Try beginning each prayer with words of gratitude. Tell the Lord specific things that bring you joy. And look for His hand in the challenges you face.

CHAPTER 4

HOW TO KEEP COOL WHEN THINGS GET HOT

Pursue peace with all people.

—*Hebrews 12:14*

The twentieth century was the most murderous century in recorded history. War alone was directly or indirectly responsible for the deaths of 187 million people. That century saw almost unbroken war—165 organized armed conflicts, with only a few brief periods without them. The world's political leaders formed the League of Nations and then the United Nations to maintain peace, but their efforts failed. It reminds me of the texts: " 'They have healed the hurt of the daughter of My people slightly, / Saying, "Peace, peace!" / When there is no peace' " (Jeremiah 8:11), and " 'when you hear of wars and rumors of wars, do not be troubled; for such things must happen, but the end is not yet' " (Mark 13:7).

Not only are people looking for international peace, they're looking for personal peace as well. Not long ago, I saw an ad for a book titled *Buddhism for Busy People*. The advertisement assured that with the proper technique, purchasers can experience peace. The same author has written another book, titled *Hurry Up and Meditate: Your Starter Kit for Inner Peace and Better Health*.

Once, in an airport, I struck up a conversation with a woman who was sitting next to me. She told me she was returning from a retreat and then began to tell me what it had been about. She emphasized several times that she wasn't a Buddhist. I was wondering what this had to do with anything until she mentioned some of the things the instructor had tried to teach. She said that one of the things the attendees learned was how to think about nothing. No, I didn't say that right. They were taught how not to think about anything—there is a difference! I didn't say anything to her, but it occurred to me that it would be impossible not to think about anything. How could you respond if your teacher were to ask if your mind was empty? And so the search for peace goes on.

The opposite of turning off one's mind and not thinking about anything is to have one's mind in gear and to be constantly worrying about everything. I like the comparison that suggests worry is like a rocking chair: it gives us something to do, but it never gets us anywhere.

I must confess that I'm a person who's inclined to worry. When I was thirty-seven years old, I developed an ulcer and lost half of my blood. This shows how intensely I live life. Things have been much better in the years since, but I'm still not sure what to think when someone says, "Don't worry." The truth is, not worrying is easier for some people than for others.

Things would be much improved for people like me who tend to worry, if we would just remember the words of our Lord: " 'Do not worry about tomorrow, for tomorrow will worry about its own things. Sufficient for the day is its own trouble' " (Matthew 6:34). In other words, Jesus was saying that we should live one day at a time.

According to my thesaurus, the word *worry* means, among other things, "to be concerned or to be anxious." Now if this is the case, there is probably nothing wrong with being worried—that is, concerned or anxious—when one of our grandchildren is sick. But if there's a worry that's appropriate, there's also a worry that's toxic. Those who are concerned when the grandchildren are sick have an appropriate worry. Those who worry that one of these days the healthy grandchildren may become sick have toxic worry. But even appropriate worry will be greatly reduced as we learn to trust God and live one day at a time. Most people have a tendency to live in the past, the present, and the future all at once.

AFRAID OF THE DARK?

A natural extension of worry and anxiety is fear. Were you ever afraid of the dark? For a while I was. I also remember several incidences when other things frightened me. I must have been eight or nine years old when I stepped on a long blacksnake while I was walking barefoot through a field. Do I need to say more? I knew the snake wasn't poisonous, but he began to thrash around, banging into my legs. I don't know how high I jumped or how fast I ran, but, needless to say, the whole thing scared me nearly to death.

Another time I was really scared was the summer Dad and Mom set up twin beds in our one-car garage. (In those days, a two-car garage wasn't necessary because no one had two cars!) Our house was small for the six of us, so my younger brother and I slept in the garage that summer. Our tomcat Boots slept on the floor beside us. My parents left the back door of the garage open for ventilation, covering the opening with a sheer curtain to keep the mosquitoes out.

One night when I was sound asleep, Boots heard another tom just outside the door. He took a flying leap across my chest toward the door while growling the way tomcats do. Can you imagine waking up, hearing the growl, and feeling something brush across your chest? Even after all these years, I still can feel the tears of fright running down my cheeks!

Like worry, there is appropriate fear and inappropriate fear. Natural fear can be caused by something that happens all of a sudden, as in the case of stepping barefoot on a blacksnake or having a cat jump across your chest in the middle of the night. But then there is the fear of something that hasn't happened yet and might not happen. "I don't know what's going to happen to me," "I'm afraid that—" This is fear that comes from toxic worry, and we have all experienced it at one time or another.

When I lived in South America, a friend gave me a one-hundred-dollar bill he had picked up somewhere. But don't call me lucky—the money wasn't genuine, it was a counterfeit. The world offers a counterfeit peace that consists of attempting to escape from reality and drop out of life. People try to get through the day with the aid of coffee, pills, alcohol, cigarettes, or other crutches. But that's not the way to obtain peace. When we look to the Lord, even in our toxic worry and fear, He doesn't leave us. There are wonderfully comforting texts for those of us who may be passing through the valley of deepest gloom. My favorite is, "Yea, though I walk through the valley of the shadow of death, / I will fear no evil; / For You are with me; / Your rod and Your staff, they comfort me" (Psalm 23:4).

Here are some others:

- "In God I have put my trust; / I will not be afraid. / What can man do to me?" (Psalm 56:11). Notice the word *trust*?
- "You shall not be afraid of the terror by night, / Nor of the arrow that flies by day" (Psalm 91:5).
- "He will not be afraid of evil tidings; / His heart is steadfast, trusting in the LORD" (Psalm 112:7). In this text, as in the first one above, it is trust in God that casts out fear.
- "When you lie down, you will not be afraid; / Yes, you will lie down and your sleep will be sweet" (Proverbs 3:24).

- " ' "Fear not, for I am with you; / Be not dismayed, for I am your God. / I will strengthen you, / Yes, I will help you, / I will uphold you with My righteous right hand" ' " (Isaiah 41:10).

The secret to living one day at a time is trusting in God. "Trust in the LORD with all your heart, / And lean not on your own understanding; / In all your ways acknowledge Him, / And He shall direct your paths" (Proverbs 3:5, 6). We obtain peace when we trust in God; it is a fruit of the Spirit.

You remember the story of the storm on Lake Galilee. The disciples thought their lives were about to end, but Jesus was sleeping through it. He wasn't sleeping in a first-class cabin on the *Queen Mary,* so He couldn't have been very comfortable—bouncing around on the waves, drenched with spray, the disciples hollering over the roar of the wind and waves. But Jesus slept because He trusted His Father in heaven, and because He trusted, He had peace.

Recently I read some very interesting things about ships relevant to the subject of peace. Ships have come a long way since the Vikings sailed the seas and the Pilgrims arrived on the *Mayflower.* Although I have never been on a really big ship, my wife and I and our three children spent a month on a small freighter named *The Steel Director;* we were sailing to Pakistan to be missionaries. (During the first ten days, we sailed through a nonstop storm on the Atlantic Ocean!) The ship wasn't very big; it couldn't have been a hundred feet long. Compare that to the *Queen Mary,* at 963 feet long (293 meters); the *Norway,* at 1,035 feet (315 meters); and the USS *Nimitz,* at 1,092 feet (332 meters).

These days, large ships have a bow-mounted pitch stabilizer—a rigid support structure attached to the bow—and one or more horizontally pivoted flaps that resist the up-and-down movement of the bow. The really big ships also have gyroscopes that reduce the side-to-side rolling in rough weather. These mechanisms that stabilize ships in rough seas helped me understand the role that God's gift of peace has in the storms of life. When we have peace from above, life will still have its ups and downs, but we won't capsize.

THE SHADOW OF DEATH

People who are passing through times of grief especially need peace—and sooner or later, we'll all experience grief. If you haven't yet, you just haven't lived long enough. "The days of our lives are seventy years; / And if by reason of strength they are eighty years, / Yet their boast is only labor and sorrow; / For it is soon cut off, and we fly away" (Psalm 90:10).

In many weddings, the minister asks, "Do you promise to love, honor, and cherish, in sickness and in health, for better or for worse, till death do you part?" Of course, the couple says, "I do." But little do they think at the time that down the line there will be hardship and sickness and that one or the other of them is going to be a widow or a widower. Those who have learned to trust the Lord find peace even in these tough times.

Some have said that there is no greater grief than the loss of a child. In 1873, two years after the great Chicago fire, Horatio Spafford, a prosperous lawyer and devout Presbyterian Church elder, and his wife, Anna, were living comfortably with their four young daughters in that city. The family decided to vacation with friends in Europe. However, at the last moment, Horatio was detained by business that required his attention, so Anna and the girls went on ahead to Paris, sailing on the ocean liner SS *Ville du Havre*. On November 21, the luxury steamer was rammed amidships by a British vessel and sank within minutes. Anna was picked up unconscious on a floating spar, but the four girls had drowned. Nine days after the shipwreck, the vessel carrying the survivors landed in Cardiff, Wales, and Anna cabled Horatio, "Saved alone. What shall I do?"

Upon receiving Anna's telegram, Horatio immediately left Chicago to bring his wife home. On the Atlantic crossing, the captain of the ship called Horatio to his cabin to tell him that they were nearing the place where his four daughters had perished. As the ship passed over their watery grave, Horatio wrote the words to the hymn we still sing:

> When peace like a river, attendeth my way,
> When sorrows like sea billows roll—
> Whatever my lot, thou hast taught me to say,
> It is well, it is well with my soul.[1]

Perhaps the peace we need most is peace at home. Since our beginnings as a church, we have known that in the last days the Sabbath would be the object of Satan's attack. However, we need to remind ourselves that at the end of the Creation week, God established two institutions, not just one: He established the home as well as the Sabbath. Little could we have imagined that at the end of this earth's history, the devil would bring all of his forces to bear not only against the Sabbath but also against the home, the family.

We have all learned by experience that the most difficult place to be a Christian is at home. Yet "home is to be the center of the purest and most elevated affections. Peace, harmony, affection, and happiness should be perseveringly cherished every day, until these precious things abide in the hearts of those who compose the family."[2]

At this point you may be thinking, *I believe this is true. But Pastor O'Ffill, you don't know my home. You don't understand what it's like. At our house, it seems as though we're constantly fighting. What can I do?*

The apostle Paul tells us what to do when we're passing through difficult circumstances with difficult people, even when they happen to be members of our own family. He counsels, "If it is possible, as much as depends on you, live peaceably with all men" (Romans 12:18). Those who have the peace that passes understanding don't say, "I will be peaceful if you will be peaceful."

I like the Serenity Prayer, by Reinhold Niebuhr. It's especially helpful for us to remember when there are difficulties at home:

> God grant me the serenity
> to accept the things I cannot change;
> courage to change the things I can;
> and wisdom to know the difference.

PEACE IN THE CHURCH

Of course when there is no peace in the home, sooner or later this lack will be reflected in the church. After all, the church is the sum of its individual families. It is inevitable that within the church family there will be disagreements. Sometimes the only way is to agree to disagree. Even the apostles had sharp contentions among them, but they carried on with their commission of preaching the gospel to the whole world. "Those who take Christ at His word, and surrender their souls to His keeping, their lives to His ordering, will find peace and quietude."[3] Whether at home or in the church, the promise to those who do their best to maintain peace and quietude is " 'Blessed are the peacemakers, / For they shall be called sons of God' " (Matthew 5:9).

Receiving peace is not like getting a package from UPS at the front door. Peace, like all the other fruit of the Spirit, must be sought after (Matthew 7:7). Those who are filled with the Holy Spirit are those who " 'hunger and thirst for righteousness' " (Matthew 5:6).

Francis of Assisi, born in 1181, said it so beautifully:

> Lord, make me an instrument of Thy peace;
> where there is hatred, let me sow love;
> where there is injury, pardon;

where there is doubt, faith;
where there is despair, hope;
where there is darkness, light;
and where there is sadness, joy.
O Divine Master,
grant that I may not so much seek to be consoled as to
    console;
to be understood, as to understand;
to be loved, as to love;
for it is in giving that we receive,
it is in pardoning that we are pardoned,
and it is in dying that we are born to eternal life.

My mom and dad are gone now, but I remember when they were young. Dad was tall and handsome, and Mother was pretty, with black hair and blue eyes. They often sang duets at church. One of the songs I remember them singing was written in the nineteenth century by Warren Cornell at a Methodist camp meeting near East Bend, Wisconsin. Its title is "Wonderful Peace." The words of the chorus are

Peace! peace! wonderful peace,
Coming down from the Father above;
Sweep over my spirit forever, I pray,
In fathomless billows of love.

True peace is not something that is always somewhere else— something that makes us wish, "If I could only find it"! True peace grows within our hearts as a fruit of the Spirit. So then it's with us wherever we are. It's important that we remember this, because with Jesus, it's what we're becoming that counts.

1. The story of the events leading up to the writing of this hymn is told in a Library of Congress exhibit on the American Colony in Jerusalem; see http://www.loc.gov/exhibits/americancolony/amcolony-family.html.

2. Ellen G. White, *The Adventist Home* (Nashville: Southern Publishing Association, 1952), 195.

3. White, *The Desire of Ages* (Mountain View, Calif.: Pacific Press® Publishing Association, 1940), 331.

Thinking It Over

1. Identify a specific place in your life where there is a storm.

2. Jesus didn't flee from the storms that swirled around His life; He kept on keeping on. What do you think enabled Him to do this?

3. Remember the Serenity Prayer—especially the part that says "courage to change the things I can." What might some of those "things" be in your life?

CHAPTER 5

HOW TO HAVE THE PATIENCE TO HAVE PATIENCE

You have need of endurance [patience], so that after you have done the will of God, you may receive the promise.

—*Hebrews 10:36*

I like this quote by Paul Sweeney: "How can a society that exists on instant mashed potatoes, packaged cake mixes, frozen dinners, and instant cameras teach patience to its young?"

Perhaps you've heard of the lady who prayed, "Lord, I want patience, and I want it NOW!"

Jeff was a guy who, by his own admission, flew off the handle fast and furiously. "I can't keep reacting this way," he confided to me. "I need to learn how to be patient. How can I do it?"

"Jeff," I replied with tongue in cheek, "you can learn to be patient, but it's going to take patience!"

It's true. Patience, like the other fruit of the Spirit, is not something that you get on demand.

I was riding in a yellow cab in midtown Manhattan. Just to make conversation, I asked the driver how many miles he was able to put on a typical cab. His answer: "I expect to get about two hundred fifty thousand."

Now, I'm not a car dealer or a mechanic, but to me that sounded pretty good. I figured it was a lot for a vehicle that's driven in the city all day, every day. Curiosity overcame social correctness and I came right out and asked him, "So, how do you get that many miles?"

His answer was short and to the point: "I keep the engine cool and slippery."

I wish my friend who needs patience had been there to hear what the cab driver said, because it has a lot to do with what patience does for us. I believe it's safe to say that patience is the Spirit-given quality that keeps us cool when things don't go as we think they ought. And, like the motor oil that keeps in suspension impurities within the engine, patience holds in suspension the kinds of things that make us fly off the handle. Patience, then, is the element in the fruit of the Spirit that keeps the other elements running like a smooth, well-tuned engine.

Jeff isn't the only one who needs patience. I don't know about you, but I need it all day, every day. But it's one thing to say we need to be patient; it's another to know what patience is and how it works in the life of the Christian.

To understand the meaning of a significant spiritual concept, we need to find the places in Scripture where the word is used. So find a Bible with a good concordance. A little hint: There is another word in Scripture that is used interchangeably with patience, and that is *long-suffering*.

Think for a moment about the story of Moses on Mount Sinai. (The story is found in Exodus 33:18–34:6.) There on the mountain Moses asked God to show him His glory. When we think of the glory of God, we think of the glorious light and all the myriad of angels that surround Him. But on that day so long ago, God showed Moses—and so has shown us—a true picture of His glory. His glory is simply and wonderfully Himself. Not fire, light, angels, thunderings, or earthquakes—His glory is what He is. So when God had hidden Moses in a sheltered place, He passed before him and proclaimed, "The LORD, the LORD God, merciful and gracious, longsuffering, and abundant in goodness and truth" (verse 6, KJV).

When you're asked to describe a person you don't know personally, you probably describe the way that person looks—tall, short, brown eyes, blue eyes, curly hair, straight hair, and so forth. On the other hand, when asked to describe someone you love, you probably describe that person's personality or character—kind, fun-loving, cheerful, melancholy, and so forth. The glory of the Lord is not what He looks like but who He is. Moses wanted to see God's face; God showed him His heart.

I'm going to ask you a personal question: How would your family describe *you*? Loving, merciful, patient, and kind—or . . . ?

Believe it or not, we can actually begin to understand what patience is by learning what it isn't, or what its opposite—impatience—is.

WHOSE WAY IS BEST?

Impatience is saying to God that our way is the best way. A case in point is the experience of Abraham (Genesis 15). God had promised to give Abraham and Sarah a son. Abraham became impatient. He figured that what God had promised was now beyond impossible and that if it was going to happen, it would have to happen Abraham's way. So he took Hagar as his wife, and they had a son and named him Ishmael. Abraham's impatience changed the course of history.

Exodus contains another example of impatience—in this case, the impatience not of one person but of many: "When the people saw that Moses delayed coming down from the mountain, the people gathered together to Aaron, and said to him, 'Come, make us gods that shall go before us; for as for this Moses, the man who brought us up out of the land of Egypt, we do not know what has become of him' " (Exodus 32:1). When Moses didn't come down from Mount Sinai when the children of Israel thought he should, they became impatient and decided to take matters into their own hands and made themselves a golden calf to worship.

In the Garden of Gethsemane, the apostle Peter became impatient and angry. I suppose he was impatient that Jesus didn't stand up for Himself and destroy the soldiers who had come to arrest Him, and Peter was angry at himself because he had fallen asleep. No doubt he was trying to impress our Lord into believing that while he may have been sleeping before, he was wide awake now and would step in and take care of this crowd if Jesus wasn't going to. "Then Simon Peter, having a sword, drew it and struck the high priest's servant, and cut off his right ear. The servant's name was Malchus. So Jesus said to Peter, 'Put your sword into the sheath. Shall I not drink the cup which My Father has given Me?'" (John 18:10, 11).

In addition to real-life experiences, Jesus told several parables of what happens when we become impatient. One parable is the story of ten young women (Matthew 25:1–10).

Have you ever wondered why the young women would be waiting for the bridegroom? Usually we connect bridesmaids with the bride and groomsmen with the groom. It seems unlikely that girls would be waiting for a bridegroom. But after living for a number of years in Southern Asia, I understand the connection, because in that part of the world, the center of attention at a wedding is the groom, not the bride. The groom wears the fancy clothes and sometimes even the veil. Often the bride is practically invisible, covered from head to toe. So it was very normal that the young women in the parable were "groomsmaids"!

When the groom didn't show up at the time the wedding party thought he should, the attendants became impatient and decided they had time enough to take a nap. But the groom came while they slept, and you know the rest of the story: half of them missed the wedding. In other words, Jesus was warning that many people who claim to believe in Him will not be ready for His advent.

Jesus told another interesting story about the consequence of impatience. In this story, a boss didn't come home when the workers expected him to, and they became impatient. Jesus warned His hearers: " 'If that servant says in his heart, "My master is delaying his coming," and begins to beat the male and female servants, and to eat and drink and be drunk, the master of that servant will come on a day when he is not looking for him, and at an hour when he is not aware, and will cut him in two and appoint him his portion with the unbelievers' " (Luke 12:45, 46).

In this parable there is, first, expectation. Then impatience arises, and finally, people experience the consequences. There is a lesson that we individually and as a church should learn from this story. The Seventh-day Adventist Church was born after the Great Disappointment that resulted when Jesus didn't come as expected on October 22, 1844. But we have suffered another great disappointment even more significant than the first. Here's why I say this. My dad believed that Jesus would come before he could finish college. To him, there wouldn't even be time to get married and have a family. But Jesus didn't come, and now Dad's generation has practically passed off the scene. It appears to us that our Lord has delayed His coming. The danger now is not just that we go to sleep but, even worse, that we beat up on each other and begin to live the way of the world. Will we, like the groomsmaids, be taken by surprise?

Friend, the ultimate test of our patience is waiting for the coming of Jesus. In the short term, impatience seriously cripples our commitment to God, and in the long term—which very well may be shorter than we think—we run the risk of losing our salvation.

PUTTING OTHERS IN THEIR PLACE

Impatience is a way of judging each other and putting each other down. Impatience pays no attention to the golden rule, which says we should do to others as we would have them do to us.

Peter once asked Jesus how many times we should forgive each other. The Pharisees taught that seven times was enough. That meant they had to be patient with each other only until they got fed up. Jesus taught the true meaning not only of forgiveness but of patience when He said we should be patient all the time: "seventy times seven." In other words, beyond counting.

Patience doesn't stand back with a come-what-may attitude, but neither does it fly off the handle. Patience knows the meaning of the words, "My beloved brethren, let every man be swift to hear, slow to speak, slow to wrath; for the wrath of man does not produce the righteousness of God" (James 1:19, 20).

Anger is a natural consequence of impatience. When we lose our patience, we tend to lose our temper. In this imperfect world full of imperfect people, there are abundant reasons to be angry. If only a reason were a legitimate excuse! But the people on whom the Holy Spirit is bestowing the fruit of patience won't be looking for reasons to justify their anger.

I hope you're not thinking that I'm trying to oversimplify something that's very complicated. Yes, I realize there are many problems in the family and even in the church. But let's be patient. As the fruit of patience grows, we'll find that many of the more complicated details of our relationships with each other will diminish—and many will even disappear.

We live in Central Florida. On several occasions, when we've bought a pineapple from the supermarket, I've cut off the green stalk and planted it in our flower garden. The stalk usually takes root quickly, and before long, I have a nice-looking pineapple plant. I read something on the Internet about growing pineapples that I already had learned by experience. The Web site advised, "Patience is the key to successfully growing a pineapple plant. It often takes two years or more for a plant to bear fruit in peak growing conditions." Pineapples aren't the only things that take patience to grow. Mushrooms may come up in a day or two, but it takes generations to grow a redwood. Ralph Waldo Emerson said, "Adopt the pace of nature: her secret is patience."

PATIENCE GROWS THROUGH SUFFERING

The Bible tells us that sometimes patience can develop as a result of suffering. I don't know about you, but I often pray for patience, but am reluctant to go through what it takes to get it. This is like praying out of two sides of our mouths. On one side we ask the Lord to give us patience, and on the other side we pray that all will be well and our path will be smooth. Do you see how one prayer cancels out the other?

How does patience grow in bad times? The apostle James explains it this way: "My brethren, count it all joy when you fall into various trials, knowing that the testing of your faith produces patience. But let patience have its perfect work, that you may be perfect and complete, lacking nothing" (James 1:2–4). By the way, in the verse above, the word *trials* is sometimes translated *divers temptations*. And we can understand this, because the trials that sooner or later we must all endure are temptations, and temptations are certainly trials. Our trials are temptations because when we're passing through them, we're tempted to do some of the things mentioned earlier in this chapter. (Remember my friend Jeff?) I especially like this part from that verse in James: "But let patience have its perfect work, that you may be perfect and complete, lacking nothing."

The apostle Paul knew what it was like to have trials: He wrote, "In all things [I and my companions are] approving ourselves as ministers of God, in much patience, in afflictions, in necessities, in distresses" (2 Corinthians 6:4, KJV). In fact, he said, "We . . . glory in tribulations, knowing that tribulation produces perseverance" (Romans 5:3).

One of the biggest tribulations in my life is to have a child who is out of the church. And I know I'm not alone. Sometimes I become very impatient with God. I plead with Him to do something *now*. It hasn't happened yet, and I don't know how long it will take, but one thing I know: that in the meantime the seed of patience is growing in my heart. I am learning to understand that God is the same today as He was when He showed Himself to Moses so long ago—that He is long-suffering.

As you read this chapter, you may be suffering from an illness or a disability. Maybe you've lost a spouse and are alone. Here's a promise that will sustain you as you grow the fruit of patience: "No temptation [trial] has overtaken you except such as is common to man; but God is faithful, who will not allow you to be tempted beyond what you are able, but with the temptation will also make the way of escape, that you may be able to bear it" (1 Corinthians 10:13).

Patience won't get us out of our problems, but it is a wonderful gift, a fruit of the Spirit, that God gives us to be able to get through those problems. In the meantime, "since we are surrounded by so great a cloud of witnesses [read: we are not alone], let us lay aside every weight [trusting in our own way], and the sin which so easily ensnares us [anger], and let us run with endurance [patience] the race that is set before us" (Hebrews 12:1).

Of those who are saved at the end of time, it is written: "Here is the patience of the saints" (Revelation 14:12). This text is a comfort to me, because it means that He who has begun a good work in us (patience) will finish it and will give us strength all along the way. And so we must let patience have its perfect work, that we may be like our heavenly Father. "The LORD passed by before him and proclaimed, the LORD, the LORD God, . . . longsuffering and abundant in goodness and truth" (KJV).

THINKING IT OVER

1. Would you classify yourself as being patient or impatient?
2. What's testing your patience the most right now?
3. Patience is a gift of the Spirit. What can you do to help this gift grow within you? What kinds of things will keep it from growing?

CHAPTER 6

How to Get Back at Someone Without Going Backward

Be kind to one another.

—Ephesians 4:32

For years my hobby was tropical fish. So I was interested when I came across the story of a man whose children had been pleading with him to buy some goldfish. But having goldfish is not as simple as just picking out the ones the kids liked best. There's the matter of a fish tank, fish food, and a filter to keep the water clean. The filter is operated by a small air pump, which aerates the water as well.

The man happened to mention to a friend that he was thinking of buying some goldfish and needed an aquarium. His friend said he had one that he wasn't using anymore and he would sell it for ten dollars. So, they struck a deal.

The aquarium hadn't been used for a while, so the new hobbyist cleaned it up with soap and water. Then he and his kids went to a pet store and bought some goldfish, along with the other things they needed. They set up the aquarium with gravel, filter, and fish. However, several days later, much to the dismay of the children, the fish died. As near as the man could figure it, the problem was that he hadn't rinsed out the soap thoroughly enough when he cleaned the tank. It was a case of the cure being worse than the disease!

As we continue to study the fruit of the Spirit, we begin to realize that what we thought was the right way to do things is often the wrong way. It reminds me of two texts: "There is a way that seems right to a man, / But its end is the way of death" (Proverbs 16:25), and " 'As the heavens are higher than the earth, / So are My ways higher than your ways, / And My thoughts than your thoughts' " (Isaiah 55:9). As we will see, the next fruit bears this out.

The Hebrew word is *chesed* (pronounced KHE-*ced*), and the Greek word is *chrēstotēs* (pronounced *chray-*STO-*tays*). In some Bibles, the word is translated "gentleness"; in others, "kindness." This makes sense because gentleness is being kind, and kindness is being gentle.

The fruit of the Spirit is love, but love by itself is invisible. It's kindness that unpacks love—gives it arms and legs, hands and feet. Kindness brings love out into the open; it makes it materialize. Kindness is the window through which love can be seen.

In the Sermon on the Mount, Jesus said that His followers would be the salt of the earth (Matthew 5:13). I never fully understood what Jesus meant when He said that if the salt has lost its savor, it might as well be thrown away. I thought salt was always salty. But now I understand that Jesus was using a supposition; in other words, He was saying, "Suppose that salt should lose its savor . . ." If salt isn't doing what it's suppose to do—that is, giving flavor and preserving—it's useless. So when Jesus says that we are the salt of the earth, He's telling us that if we're not giving flavor to the world and doing our part to preserve (to save) souls, we have no purpose—we're useless, good for nothing.

One day a group of Christians decided to have a meeting over lunch at a restaurant. When the waitress came to take their order, they told her what they wanted but hardly looked at her, and, in fact, throughout the entire meal they hardly noticed her. She might as well have been invisible. The group's conversation had made it clear that they were religious people. Not a Christian herself, the waitress probably thought, *So this is what Christians are like!*

When she brought the dessert, one of the committee members didn't receive an item he had ordered, and he told the waitress in no uncertain terms that he wanted it brought immediately. And when the group finished eating, they tossed a dollar tip and a tract on how to accept Jesus on the table. Again, she probably thought to herself, *So this is what Christians are like!*

Sometimes when I travel or even when I go shopping, much to the embarrassment of my wife, I go out of my way to recognize and joke with the cashiers, the flight attendants, and others who are there to help. More than once they have expressed how much they appreciate being recognized and treated kindly. They say that much of the time customers talk to them only when they have a complaint.

Kindness makes love real and, as a consequence, makes the gospel attractive. It only stands to reason that Christian witnessing must begin with kindness. We show the love of Jesus by being kind. There's a hymn we used to sing more than we do now. Some of the words say,

> If you cannot sing like angels,
> If you cannot preach like Paul,
> You can tell the love of Jesus,
> And say He died for all.

We can do this by simply being kind.

BROAD-SPECTRUM KINDNESS

Kindness arises from who we are. It's not meant to be directed just to some but to everyone. It is broad spectrum—it enables us to always be the same regardless of where we are or who we're with. It feels what others feel—their joy or their sadness. It is evidenced in both the up times and the down times. Kind people will celebrate along with others when they have good reason to celebrate; and when others are hurting, kind people will show compassion (Romans 12:15).

The apostle James uses a little satire but at the same time is serious when he poses the supposition of a brother or sister who comes along having hardly any clothes to keep them warm and who hasn't eaten for several days, and someone says to them in effect, "Be seeing you. I hope you find some warm clothes and something to eat. Good luck!" James asks, "What good is that?" (see James 2:15, 16).

John the beloved agrees: "Whoever has this world's goods, and sees his brother in need, and shuts up his heart from him, how does the love of God abide in him? My little children, let us not love in word or in tongue, but in deed and in truth" (1 John 3:17, 18). Kindness is love expressing itself in deeds.

Once when the regular Sabbath School teacher didn't show up, I volunteered to teach the Sabbath School lesson. As I began the class, I noticed a young man and his mother sitting to my left. The young man was listening with rapt attention and seemed to be drinking in all I was saying. He was obviously a visitor, and as we welcomed everyone, he told us his name was Joshua. By the way he dressed, I could see that he was from what some might call the working class or may have even been out of work.

After the class, I introduced myself to him. As we talked, I couldn't help but notice that his front teeth were badly stained. I confess with regret that this began to affect the way I related to him. Why is it that when a person doesn't look the way we think they should, we have negative feelings? Later, I felt ashamed of myself. My wife and I discussed this incident and agreed that the next Sabbath we would get to know him better.

The entire experience reminded me of James 2:1–4: "My brethren, do not hold the faith of our Lord Jesus Christ, the Lord of glory, with partiality. For if there should come into your assembly a man with gold rings, in fine apparel, and there should also come in a poor man in filthy clothes, and you pay attention to the one wearing the fine clothes and say to him, 'You sit here in a good place,' and say to the poor man, 'You stand there,' or, 'Sit here at my footstool,' have you not shown partiality among yourselves, and become judges with evil thoughts?"

Kindness is no respecter of persons. Kindness practices what the Bible preaches—it shares with a brother or sister. Kindness cuts the grass or shovels the snow for an elderly neighbor. Kindness drives the car patiently and carefully. Kindness *gently* warns a friend who is heading in the wrong direction. In times of discouragement, kindness offers encouraging words. It lends a helping hand.

There are things kindness refuses to do. Kindness won't gossip. It refuses to cheat. Kindness won't make fun of others; it won't insult others. Kindness doesn't have time to waste on pouting or jealousy.

Sad to say, sometimes we withhold kindness for the simple reason that we're selfish and don't want to admit it. Other times we choose to withhold kindness because someone has been unkind to us. Kindness never treats someone badly just because they have treated us badly. Jesus was kind even to those who were unkind to Him. He says, " 'Love your enemies, do good, and lend, hoping for nothing in return; and your reward will be great, and you will be sons of the Most High. For He is kind to the unthankful and evil' " (Luke 6:35).

The truly kind person is one who doesn't flinch at the cost of extending kindness. This is the quality of kindness that characterizes God our Father. He cares even when we don't care. He suffers for us even when we'd rather not be bothered. "God demonstrates His own love toward us, in that while we were still sinners, Christ died for us" (Romans 5:8).

It's wrong to be kind to others expecting that they will reciprocate. It's far better to do what Jesus would do and then leave the results entirely in God's hands. The fact is that no matter what we may do or how much we may put ourselves out, some people won't show any appreciation at all. So unless our kindness is like the kindness of Jesus, we'll end up disillusioned and discouraged.

WHEN IT'S HARD TO BE KIND

We all have to admit there are times when it's hard to be kind. We work hard all day, and when we get home we may find our spouse tired and the children complaining. It's hard to be kind at work, too, when someone is especially obnoxious. For that matter, it's difficult to be kind even at church when someone disagrees with us or is critical.

An old adage says, "All that glitters is not gold." The same thing is true of kindness. There's a kindness that is disingenuous. Sometimes we see what may look like kindness only to discover later that it's only a counterfeit kindness used to manipulate others. The Bible gives several examples of what appeared to be kindness but was used for a nefarious end. Jacob showed kindness to his brother, Esau, and in the process took away his birthright (Genesis 25:29–34). Jael treated Sisera to a bottle of milk and a few moments of rest and then took his life as he slept (Judges 4:18–21). Delilah spoke words of love to Samson and then betrayed him to his enemies (Judges 16:4–21). Genuine kindness doesn't have a hidden agenda.

In the workplace, it's baffling how on a one-to-one basis, a fellow employee can appear to be down to earth and just one of the buddies, yet at a committee table act entirely different! Before, it was one for all and all for one, but in committee, it often becomes every person for himself or herself. At times one can almost see the wheels of the mind turning as all the committee members try to gain the advantage and protect their turf.

But we shouldn't be surprised. Power often becomes impersonal and even cold. Often, when people rise to a new position, they're tempted to become less kind. So, genuine kindness is tested when we're suddenly thrust into a position of power. Abraham Lincoln was a kind president who refused to heed the calls for him to crush the South. He stood his ground, demanding "malice toward none and charity for all." Nothing is so strong or powerful as true kindness.

It has been said that the place where it's most difficult to be kind is at home. At the office one day, a fellow was heard to say wearily, "I can't wait to get home at night. I get so tired of being kind all day." When I conduct seminars on the home, I often pose the questions: "How long would we last on the job if we treated our boss the way we treat each other at home? What will our homes be like when we are truly kind?"

I once heard a mother say, "My word is law!" And so it is—yet as parents we can be so anxious to run a tight ship that we sink the ship. In our families we say we love each other, and I'm sure we do, yet love must express itself in kindness. Surely we must be aware that unkindness extinguishes love.

> In order to have the proper control of our children, we must manifest a spirit of gentleness and of meekness and of long-suffering. We do not want to have a faultfinding, fretful, scolding spirit. If we teach them to have a spirit of gentleness, we must have a spirit of gentleness ourselves; . . . if we would have them manifest a spirit of love toward us, we must manifest a gentle, loving spirit toward them. But at the same time there need be no weakness or unwise indulgence on the part of parents. The mother must have firmness and decision. She must be as firm as a rock, and not swerve from the right. Her laws and rules should be carried out at all times and under all hazards, but she can do this with all gentleness and meekness. . . . The children will grow up God-fearing men and women.[1]

We must also beware of what could be called phony kindness. It's not kindness for a parent to allow a child to do wrong deliberately. To indulge a child's every whim and desire is not kindness. Sometimes a parent or grandparent may smile and tell how they spoil their children or grandchildren. But to overlook a wrong, to brush it aside, to sweep it under the carpet, is not kindness. It costs something to care.

NOT LIKE JONAH

When I was a Seminary student at Andrews University, I noticed in the South Bend newspaper's weekend edition that from time to time a church would advertise services in which a child preacher was scheduled to speak, usually on a Sunday evening. The idea of hearing a six- or seven-year-old child preach sounded interesting to several of us Seminary students, so one Sunday evening in midwinter, four of us squeezed into my Renault Dauphine (about the size of a Volkswagen Beetle) and through the snowy night went to hear what the little preacher had to say.

He couldn't have been more than six years old. His sermon was about prayer. The Bible illustration was Jonah and the whale. I will never forget his words as he finished his sermon. He said, "And so Jonah prayed. The whale came up on the beach, stuck out his tongue, and Jonah used it as a gangplank."

But the story of Jonah and the whale doesn't end on the beach. Chapter 2 of the story is about a selfish, unkind prophet who, after he had given the warning he was afraid to give in the first place, figured that he would sit back and watch God destroy Nineveh. But God is kind and not willing that any should perish but that all should come to repentance (2 Peter 3:9). One of the ways God expresses His love is by His kindness. "You have also given me the shield of Your salvation; / Your right hand has held me up, / Your gentleness has made me great" (Psalm 18:35).

Kindness is invariably associated with mercy. It is impossible to be kind without being merciful. Likewise, to be merciful is to be kind. The spirit of Jonah was neither.

"The wisdom that is from above is first pure, then peaceable, gentle, willing to yield, full of mercy and good fruits, without partiality and without hypocrisy" (James 3:17).

> Have you had a kindness shown?
> Pass it on;
> 'Twas not given for thee alone,
> Pass it on;
> Let it travel down the years,
> Let it wipe another's tears,
> Till in heaven the deed appears,
> Pass it on.
> —Henry Burton

---

1. Ellen G. White, *My Life Today* (Washington, D.C.: Review and Herald®, 1952), 53.

THINKING IT OVER

1. What things in our lives make it difficult to be kind? What can we do about it?
2. How could you express kindness to people you don't know?
3. Talk with a friend about how the two of you could express kindness in the church family. Share the challenge with your Sabbath School class.

CHAPTER 7

HOW GOOD IS GOOD?

The fruit of the Spirit is in all goodness, righteousness, and truth.
—*Ephesians 5:9*

I remember when my mom used to say, "Now, Dickey, Mother wants you to be a good boy." Usually when she said that, she wasn't suggesting I feed the poor and needy but more likely that I stop teasing my sister Danna or quit wiping dirt on my legs. (When I tried that one Sabbath after church, I got a switching after the sun went down!)

In this chapter, we're going to think about the fruit of the Spirit called "goodness." To get our brains in gear, I'll begin by asking several questions: What does "being good" mean to you? Does "being good" mean "doing good"? If you answer Yes, then answer this: If the devil heals someone, would that make the devil good? And finally, if someone were to ask you if you're a good person, what would you say?

Ever wonder what other people think of you? If you could listen in as a friend describes you to someone else, what would you hope to hear? Would you want your friend to describe the way you look or to say something about your great personality? Maybe you'd like your friend to discuss your intelligence or your sense of humor, or maybe your hobbies and achievements. How would you feel if all they said about you is that you're a good person? Would that be too generic? How good is good?

In all fairness, before you can answer these questions, we need a working definition of *goodness*. We use the term *good* very freely. We say: "He's a good student," "She's a good driver," "She's a good mother," "That was a good meal," and "I watched a good ball game."

In the original Anglo-Saxon, the word *good* carried the same connotation as the word *God*. One of the first little prayers that I learned was the one that goes, "God is great. God is good. Let us thank Him for this food."

God describes Himself as abounding in goodness: "The LORD passed by before him, and proclaimed, The LORD, The LORD God, merciful and gracious, longsuffering, and abundant in goodness and truth" (Exodus 34:6, KJV). God doesn't just *have* goodness or *do* goodness—God *is* good.

While God is good by nature, we definitely aren't. Our motives are mixed, and our lives are inconsistent. In spite of our earnest attempts to do right, the Bible says there is no one who does good, not even one. All have sinned and come short of the glory of God (Romans 3:12, 23).

The apostle Paul writes, "I know that nothing good lodges in me— in my unspiritual nature, I mean—for though the will to do is there, the deed is not. The good which I want to do, I fail to do; but what I do is the wrong which is against my will; and if what I do is against my will, clearly it is no longer I who am the agent, but sin that has its lodging in me. I discover this principle, then: that when I want to do the right, only the wrong is within my reach" (Romans 7:18–21, NEB).

In our sinful, selfish nature, there is no natural motivation to live God's way and to accomplish His purposes. In and of ourselves, no matter how hard we try, we can't be good. But don't put this book down yet. There's hope for us.

MORE THAN A REMODEL

A year or so ago we remodeled our living and dining rooms. We installed simulated wood flooring, put in new baseboards, took down the heavy drapery, and hung Venetian blinds. We painted the rooms and bought area rugs. But we didn't move walls or modify the basic structure; the changes we made were cosmetic and superficial. True goodness is not slapping paint on a cracked wall. It's not changing the furniture around or even buying new rugs. True goodness is not a superficial remodeling of the life—a little feeding the street people here, visiting the shut-ins there. Goodness—Godlikeness—is a deep structural change of our hearts by the Holy Spirit.

Earlier, I asked if the devil were to heal a sick person, would he be doing good? I hope you answered No to that question. In order to do something good, a person must be good; otherwise, what was done was only superficial and not intrinsically good. The fruit of the Spirit doesn't grow in from the outside but rather out from the inside. It isn't enough just to do good; it's what we are that matters. We must be good through and through. It must be the core of what we are. Jesus said that a good man brings forth good things out of the treasure of his heart (Matthew 12:35). He also said, " 'Either make the tree good and its fruit good, or else make the tree bad and its fruit bad; for a tree is known by its fruit' " (verse 33).

Like the other fruit of the Spirit, the goodness that begins to emerge from the soil of our spirits will not be our own goodness, but God's. We won't pretend to be good. There will no longer be any playacting. Instead, honest, sincere, genuine goodness becomes a supernatural outgrowth of the fruit of the Spirit of Christ. Not forced or artificial, it's the simple expression of the gracious goodness of God's Spirit at work in us.

Goodness is the result of divine power transforming the human nature. By believing in Christ, the fallen race he has redeemed may obtain that faith which works by love and purifies

64

the soul from all defilement. Then Christlike attributes appear: for by beholding Christ, men become changed into the same image from glory to glory, from character to character. Good fruit is produced. The character is fashioned after the divine similitude, and integrity, uprightness, and true benevolence are manifested toward the sinful race.[1]

Often when we talk about the importance of being good, someone will object, "But we aren't saved by works." Of course not. The genuine goodness of God is totally distinct from the so-called good works done to gain merit. *Good people* do good things! Goodness is something they do. The good fruit springs directly from the indwelling Spirit of God. The counterfeit comes from the self-centeredness of a person who is trying to impress someone. These two concepts are poles apart.

Goodness is kindness in action. Goodness is love in action—love with its hand to the plow, love with the burden on its back. Goodness is kindness expressing itself. It's a heart, a big heart, toward everybody. It's the golden rule in practice!

Goodness isn't an arm's-length kind of living either. It is a hands-on, up-close kind of living. Jesus went about doing good without asking the cost or determining the dangers. He aggressively sought out those in need of His goodness. The good things we should do for others are similar to the kinds of things Jesus would do for people.

Remember the question at the beginning of this chapter asking if you would like to be described simply as good? I hope you answered Yes. One of the grandest and most significant compliments you can ever pay a person is to call him or her good. Goodness is thoughtfulness, truthfulness, sympathy, fairness, kindness, unselfishness, helpfulness, generosity, tolerance, and forgiveness. It's food to the hungry, medicine to the sick, lenience to the bungler, forgiveness to the offender. It's a lift to the fallen, a push to the discouraged, and a song to the hopeless.

Goodness has eyes that see good in others and appreciates them. Goodness has ears that are open to hear the cry of the needy and the sobs of the brokenhearted. Goodness has a strong back upon which others can cast their burdens. Goodness has hands that are stretched out to those who are struggling and trying to stay afloat. Goodness leaves footprints for others to follow.

> The Lord has placed every human being on test and trial. He desires to prove and try us, to see if we will be good and do good in this life, to see if He can trust us with eternal riches, and make us members of the royal family, children of the heavenly King.
>
> There is no limit to the good you may do. If you make the Word of God the rule of your life, and govern your actions by its precepts, making all your purposes and exertions in the fulfilling of your duty a blessing and not a curse to others, success will crown your efforts. You have placed yourself in connection with God; you have become a channel of light to others. You are honored by becoming co-laborers with Jesus; and no higher honor can you receive than the blessed benediction from the lips of the Saviour: "Well done, good and faithful servant."[2]

GENUINE, NOT ARTIFICIAL

Sometimes what we term *goodness* is not what we might think. It's not "what you see is what you get" but rather "what you see is not necessarily what you get."

Betty and I have plants and flowers in our home. Well, not really. The plants look like palms, philodendron, ivy, and orchids, but they're artificial. We like them because we don't have to water them and make a fuss over them. Besides, they look real. But when it comes to the fruit of the Spirit, and, in this case, the fruit of goodness, artificial is completely unacceptable.

The Pharisees hated Jesus because He demanded a goodness that was heart deep, and they were willing to have a goodness that was only skin deep. I'm sure you've already figured out that it's possible to do good for the wrong reasons. We can appear to be good Christians on the outside—even give to the poor, help our neighbors, and visit the sick—but still be rotten on the inside. The Pharisees were like that.

On one occasion Jesus said to them, " 'Serpents, brood of vipers! How can you escape the condemnation of hell?' " (Matthew 23:33). And again, " 'Woe to you, scribes and Pharisees, hypocrites! For you are like whitewashed tombs which indeed appear beautiful outwardly, but inside are full of dead men's bones and all uncleanness' " (verse 27).

Christ's most devastating denunciations were directed against the phony, pious pretense of these infamous do-gooders. In plain language, He was saying, "You snakes, you stink!"

I wish I could say it wasn't so, but while most everyone will accept the idea that as followers of Jesus we must be good, not all agree as to what this means. Unfortunately, what is good and what is bad are often determined by consensus. The trend is to decide among ourselves what is good and bad, right and wrong, rather than to use the Word of God as our guide. And when discussing some biblical issue, the prevailing operatives are situation ethics and political correctness. These mean that what is good or bad depends on the situation and on the politics of the moment. Often, people who try to stand for what the Bible teaches are called judgmental or pharisaic.

There's a fast-food restaurant that advertises, "Have it your way." That slogan must never become the formula for determining what's good and what isn't. The Scriptures leave little room for doubt. "There is a way which seems right to a man, / But its end is the way of death" (Proverbs 14:12). Deciding what's right and what's wrong must not be left to a Sabbath School class or even to the pastor, because, as Jeremiah observed, " 'The heart is deceitful above all things, / And desperately wicked; /

Who can know it?' " (Jeremiah 17:9). All of this drives us to the penetrating question: Who or what do we trust to tell us what's good and what's bad?

The opinion of the crowd can't be trusted. The argument that everybody's doing it is as shabby as it sounds. Our morality must not be based on the opinion of the majority.

Then there's the psychological approach, which asks how a person feels about it. The hippies had their start on this basis. For them, goodness was determined by how they felt about something.

You may know about the "greater good" theory. I heard a story of a mother whose children were starving, so she began to sell her body to get money for food. Some felt that what she was doing was good because it was saving the lives of her children.

Sadly, even some preachers are more concerned about making their congregations feel good than they are to point them to what it means to be good. However, the only basis for true goodness is found in God's Word. David said, "Your word I have hidden in my heart, / That I might not sin against You" (Psalm 119:11).

If we're going to pray for heart goodness, we need to know what it is and what it isn't. The fundamental facts state that there must be a basis for judgment, or all of us become laws unto ourselves. Israel experienced this during the time of the judges, when "every man did that which was right in his own eyes" (Judges 17:6, KJV). But did that make it right? Hardly. The record says that "the children of Israel did evil in the eyes of the LORD" (Judges 2:11). Here we have the overwhelming proof that while a thing may seem good in our own eyes, it can be contrary to what God desires.

DAILY IMPLEMENTATION

Remember this bit of down-home advice: Reading about a dog doesn't make you one. Reading this book about the fruit of the Spirit, studying the daily Bible Study Guides, and even participating in class will do little good until, with the help of the Holy Spirit, we begin to implement it every day and everywhere in our lives.

"Therefore, my beloved, as you have always obeyed, not as in my presence only, but now much more in my absence, work out your own salvation with fear and trembling" (Philippians 2:12). This might sound like salvation by works; but the point is that a person who has salvation will be careful to live it. If we learn to do the right things and continue to practice them, we can be counted on to do right when the pressure is on, even when the odds may be against us. Daily discipline—perseverance in practice—is still the pathway to maturing in goodness of character.

In ancient China, the rulers wanted to defend their land from the barbaric hordes in the north, so they built the Great Wall. It was too high to climb over, too thick to break down, and too long to go around. Very secure. Yet during the first hundred years of the wall's existence, China was invaded three times. Was the wall a failure? Not really. Not once did the enemies manage to climb over the wall, destroy it, or go around it. How, then, did they get into China? They bribed a gate-keeper and then marched right in through a gate.

Jesus promised, " 'I give them eternal life, and they shall never perish; neither shall anyone snatch them out of My hand' " (John 10:28). No one and nothing can take us out of the hand of Jesus, but we can jump out ourselves. Similarly, the Holy Spirit offers us the gift of goodness. No one can take it from us, but we can give it up or neglect it until it withers and dies.

Someone once asked, "Which is more important, being born or staying alive?" Planting the fruit of goodness in our hearts is important. But equally important is cultivating and caring for it. It's not a weed, it's a delicate plant.

Here's something else to consider. It's unreasonable to think that a good-hearted person would do bad things. Jesus explained it this way: " 'A good tree cannot bear bad fruit, nor can a bad tree bear good fruit' " (Matthew 7:18). But needlessly exposing ourselves to badness plants the seed in our hearts. Sooner or later those who do so become bad themselves. Notice that in Galatians 5, before listing the fruit of the Spirit, Paul wrote about the works of the flesh. Too often we go blithely on our way day after day, thinking nothing about what we're feeding our minds. The old health adage "You are what you eat" applies to our minds also in the development of the fruit of goodness.

"The children of God are called upon to be representatives of Christ, showing forth the goodness and mercy of the Lord. If they but revealed His goodness from day to day, barriers would be raised around their souls against the temptations of the evil one. If they would keep in remembrance the goodness and love of God, they would be cheerful, but not vain and full of carnal mirth."[3]

John Wesley said it:

> Do all the good you can,
> By all the means you can,
> In all the ways you can,
> In all the places you can,
> In all the times you can,
> To all the people you can,
> As long as you can.

---

1. White, *My Life Today,* 54.
2. Ibid.
3. White, *Review and Herald,* January 14, 1890.

Thinking It Over

1. People seem to be substituting prayer for studying the Bible. We used to ask, "What does the Bible say?" Now we often hear "I'll pray about it" instead. What dangers does this shift in authority pose?

2. If someone were to ask the members of your family to describe you in one word, what word do you think they would use?

3. Name some things you could do that would demonstrate God's goodness to others.

CHAPTER 8

FOR BETTER OR FOR WORSE

Most men will proclaim each his own goodness, / But who can find a faithful man?

—*Proverbs 20:6*

One day Jesus asked a rhetorical question: " 'When the Son of Man comes, will He really find faith on the earth?' " (Luke 18:8). Put another way, His question might read: "When I come, will I find any who are still faithful?"

In the original languages, the word *faith* is often translated *faithfulness*. Faith is that indefinable power through which we can grasp as reality things that we haven't seen yet. Faithfulness is the working out of this belief system. When we have faith in God, we act in faithful ways. Acts of faithfulness are the threads holding our belief and behavior system together. The apostle James wrote that faith without works is dead (James 2:17). In other words, it's impossible to say you have faith if you aren't faithful.

The Bible tells the stories of the faithful and also the unfaithful. It contains accounts of people who were unfaithful but later became faithful, and it even tells the stories of people who were faithful but later became unfaithful.

At times I've wondered what reading about people who lived three thousand years ago has to do with me today. But I've come to understand that no matter when we live, the choices we make in respect to being faithful are universal and for all time. The Bible isn't a code book that has to be updated every day like television news. Though the experiences related in the Bible are from different times and different places, they're not about different people. My boss in the maintenance shop at college used to say, "People is people and folks is folks." The tests of faith for the people of God, whether past, present, or future, are basically the same. The issues that people faced two thousand years ago are the same as the ones that confront us today.

I've never been a high official in a monarchy that ruled the world as was Daniel, and I've never had to face the possibility of being thrown into a lions' den. But the basic issue, no matter the era, the situation, or its consequences, is whether or not I will be faithful.

It was Daniel's habit to pray three times a day. He wasn't trying to impress people, as did the Pharisee in Jesus' parable. Choosing not to make a public display but neither to hide himself, Daniel prayed toward Jerusalem from the window of what must have been his royal apartment. His enemies in the king's court were jealous of him and devised a plan that played on the pride of the king. For a prescribed period of time, everyone was to pray to no one but the king. The penalty for noncompliance to a royal proclamation was that the offender be thrown into a den of lions. If we had that kind of a decree hanging over our heads, we might be tempted to rationalize that we would continue to pray, but in the closet or under the bed—anywhere that wasn't as obvious as at a window. Surely a win-win solution would be to keep a low profile for the time being but continue with the devotional life.

But Daniel decided not to change his daily routine one iota. He didn't care whether he lived or died; he would remain faithful no matter what.

Here's a scenario for a modern Daniel: Your neighbors are getting together for a block party. Usually it's held on someone's front lawn. You're embarrassed to come right out and tell them that you don't drink, so you decide to go ahead and take a glass with the rest. But you never sip the drink; instead, you pour out a little when the others aren't paying attention so that the level of beer in your glass appears to go down. What would Daniel have done?

Another scenario: You're eating in a restaurant with your friends. The waiter brings the food. There's a moment of awkward silence as you look at the others out of the corner of your eye. When you're at home, you always say the blessing, but here in the restaurant . . . Well, you know how it is. You don't want to appear strange.

Little stories like this are not about a lions' den or a fiery furnace, but they are about faithfulness. Someone might ask, "Pastor O'Ffill, do you mean I'll lose my salvation if I don't say the blessing in a restaurant?" I didn't say that. But there's a text that says, " 'He who is faithful in what is least is faithful also in much; and he who is unjust in what is least is unjust also in much' " (Luke 16:10). Let's say that another way: He who is *not* faithful in little things sooner or later is not faithful in big things either. There's no difference in principle between the challenges that Daniel went through and the challenges you and I go through—minus the lions—because the challenge comes down to one question, and that is whether or not we will be faithful.

THE HANDSOME SLAVE

The Bible records another story that took place much earlier than Daniel's—the experience of Joseph. He was sold as a slave but was so faithful that Potiphar put him in charge of all that he had. Joseph was more than just a good manager. The King James Version puts it this way: "Joseph was a goodly person, and well favoured" (Genesis 39:6). I looked up the words *goodly* and *favoured* in a concordance. In Hebrew, these words don't refer to Joseph's résumé or for that matter his character. They mean that he was handsome—good looking. Potiphar's wife had a crush on him and tried to seduce him, not just once but every day.

Joseph's answer to her? " 'There is no one greater in this house than I, nor has he kept back anything from me but you, because you are his wife. How then can I do this great wickedness, and sin against God?' " (Genesis 39:9).

Joseph didn't try to give Potiphar's wife a study on what Scripture has to say about having an affair with someone else's wife. The Bible instructs us that when we're tempted to commit an act of moral impurity, we should get out of there fast. Run for our lives! "Flee sexual immorality. Every sin that a man does is outside the body, but he who commits sexual immorality sins against his own body" (1 Corinthians 6:18). It's interesting to note that Jesus carried the matter of sexual immorality to an even higher level. He said that we shouldn't even think about it! " 'Whoever looks at a woman to lust for her has already committed adultery with her in his heart' " (Matthew 5:28).

In His sermon on the mount, Jesus made a statement regarding faithfulness that many have not considered. " 'You have heard that it was said to those of old, "You shall not swear falsely, but shall perform your oaths to the Lord." But I say to you, do not swear at all: neither by heaven, for it is God's throne; nor by the earth, for it is His footstool; nor by Jerusalem, for it is the city of the great King. Nor shall you swear by your head, because you cannot make one hair white or black. But let your "Yes" be "Yes," and your "No," "No." For whatever is more than these is from the evil one' " (Matthew 5:33–37).

We have various methods of certifying that we're telling the truth; for example: "Raise your right hand. Do you swear to tell the truth, the whole truth, and nothing but the truth, so help you God?" And: "Put your right hand on the Bible and repeat after me." Sometimes it's "You must get this document notarized and file it in the courthouse."

When our Lord said that our communication should be Yes and No, He wasn't saying that we should have a vocabulary of only two words. What He meant was that those who are faithful will do what they say. They won't beat around the bush. They won't need to raise their right hand or put it on a pile of Bibles or involve a notary public. The point made is that when the faithful say Yes, they mean Yes; and when they say No, they won't need to sign on a dotted line because they're faithful to what they say.

We worked for three-and-a-half years in Pakistan. Over there, when we asked someone to do something for us, or when they offered their services, they would often add the word *inshallah* (pronounced *in-SHA-lah*), which means "if it be the will of God." The book of James suggests that when we make plans, we, too, should add "if it be the will of God" (see James 4:15). But in the Islamic Republic of Pakistan, we learned that people often used *inshallah* as an excuse not to do what they had promised. For example, when they were asked about their failure to deliver on a promise, they often would say, *"Inshallah,"* meaning, "I know I told you I would have it ready for you today, but it wasn't the will of God."

The problem of unfaithfulness isn't limited to those who have made no profession of faith in Jesus. It's evident even among "believers." It's increasingly seen as simply a weakness or family flaw. But while the character trait of faithfulness seems to be of less importance to people today than it was in the past, it has always been and will always be of great magnitude in the kingdom of heaven.

Jesus taught us that a promise is a promise. People might argue that they wouldn't have said Yes if they had known things weren't going to turn out right. Or they wouldn't have said No if they had known that things would turn out for the better. It may come as a surprise to some, but there's a text that says, "He honors those who fear the LORD; / He who swears to his own hurt and does not change" (Psalm 15:4). This means that those who serve God keep their word even if they find that it isn't to their advantage.

WEDDING PROMISES

The lack of faithfulness in our society has taken its greatest toll on marriage and the family. My dad, who was a minister, officiated at my wedding. As part of the ceremony, Dad asked me and then Betty, "Do you promise to love, honor, and cherish, for better or for worse, in sickness and in health, for richer or for poorer, till death do you part, so help you God? Do you so promise?" Of course, we said Yes. It takes a Yes to get married, but apparently, the Yes pronounced at the ceremony has little to do with being faithful to the marriage commitment later. No doubt that's why Jesus asked, "When I come, will I find faith [faithfulness] in the earth?" The implied answer is, "Not much." Those who receive their heavenly reward will not be just the ones who have faith. "Even the demons believe—and tremble!" (James 2:19). Those who are saved from any age will have one characteristic in common—at the end of the day, they were faithful.

Jesus taught lessons by telling stories. One of these stories is recorded in Matthew 25:14–30. It compares the kingdom of heaven to a man who entrusted his money managers with his liquid assets before traveling to a far country. To one he gave five talents (a measure of money), to another two talents, and to the third he gave one talent. Then he went on his journey.

When the investor returned, he called for an accounting from each of the men. He applauded the one who had invested the five talents and gained five more. He commended him for his faithfulness and said that he would now be promoted. The man who had received two talents also got a 100 percent return on the money he had been responsible for. He was congratulated for being faithful and told that he, too, would be promoted.

The money manager who had received one talent was more fearful than faithful. In fact, he was just plain cowardly. He told the investor he didn't want to take any risks, so he had put the money in a safe deposit box. When he took the talent from the box, it had actually lost value due to inflation. Of course, the Lord didn't tell the parable quite this way, but the point is the same. If, as sons and daughters of God, we're fearful instead of faithful, we'll lose not just our employment but also our place in the earth made new.

One of the most tragic events during the presidency of Ronald Reagan was a Sunday-morning terrorist bombing of the Marine barracks in Beirut, in which hundreds of Americans were killed or wounded as they slept. A few days after the tragedy, Marine Corps Commandant Paul X. Kelley visited some of the wounded soldiers, then in a Frankfurt, Germany, hospital. Among them was Corporal Jeffrey Lee Nashton, who was severely wounded. He had so many tubes running in and out of his body that a witness said he look more like a machine than a man; yet he survived. As Kelley neared Ashton, the wounded soldier struggled to move, and, racked with pain, motioned for a piece of paper and a pen. He wrote a brief note and passed it back to the commandant. On the slip of paper were the words *"Semper Fi"*— the Latin motto of the Marines; it means "Forever Faithful."

The Lord is faithful. It's His character, His glory, to be faithful. "The Lord is faithful, who will establish you and guard you from the evil one" (2 Thessalonians 3:3). "Through the LORD's mercies we are not consumed, / Because His compassions fail not. / They are new every morning; / Great is Your faithfulness" (Lamentations 3:22, 23). Those who would enter heaven will be like Him, for they shall see Him as He is (1 John 3:2).

> Great is Thy faithfulness, O God my Father,
> There is no shadow of turning with Thee,

Thou changest not, Thy compassions, they fail not;
As Thou hast been Thou forever wilt be.

Great is Thy faithfulness! Great is Thy faithfulness!
Morning by morning new mercies I see;
All I have needed Thy hand hath provided,
Great is Thy faithfulness! Lord unto me!
—Thomas Chisholm

I'm thankful that not only is our God faithful to us, but also that through the fruit of the Spirit, we will be faithful to Him. Think about it. Faithfulness can't be counterfeited. People either are faithful or they're not. It's what we are that counts.

THINKING IT OVER

1. One of the ways a spouse begins to be unfaithful is by looking at someone else. We begin to be unfaithful to Jesus when we take our eyes off Him. What other parallels of faithfulness/unfaithfulness can you come up with?

2. How can you demonstrate faithfulness to Jesus in your workplace without being like the Pharisee who prayed on the street corner?

3. The modern culture is teaching our young people to be unfaithful to their commitments, whether to God or to those who someday will be their spouses. Suppose you were a Pathfinder leader. What are some of the practical ways you could teach boys and girls the importance—the necessity—of being faithful?

CHAPTER 9

WHEN UP IS DOWN

Remind them to be subject to rulers and authorities, to obey, to be ready for every good work, to speak evil of no one, to be peaceable, gentle, showing all humility to all men.

—Titus 3:1, 2

People who spend time in the kitchen (other than the ones who simply turn on the dishwasher) can be divided into two groups—those who use dishrags and those who use sponges. My mother used to wash the dishes with a dishrag. That was before the invention of synthetic sponges. My wife usually uses a synthetic sponge. Sponges are very absorbent and are used for all kinds of things around the house. When something spills, we say, "Sponge it up."

People are like sponges. We soak up whatever we come in contact with. That's why Jesus prayed that though His disciples are in the world, they not be of the world (John 15:19). Unless we intentionally saturate ourselves with the fruit of the Spirit, we will, like sponges, absorb the world's value system. If we do, we'll inevitably think the way the world thinks, and then we'll do what the world does.

The fruit of the Spirit is a summary of the gospel according to Jesus. While there are portions of Scripture that may be difficult to understand, the teachings of Jesus aren't difficult. However, they are in and of themselves impossible to implement in our lives without the help of the Holy Spirit.

In the list of the fruit of the Spirit, meekness, or humility, is particularly difficult to obtain for two reasons: Meekness flies in the face of what we are by nature, and everything we learn from the contemporary culture tells us that in real life, it's ridiculous to be humble.

You've probably already noticed that each fruit of the Spirit is connected to the next. I'm sure there's a better way to say it, but I suggest that they're codependent. That's why neglecting to cultivate meekness and humility makes the rest of the fruit of the Spirit impossible to experience. You see, pride—which is the opposite of humility and is the mother of all sin—destroys the fruit of the Spirit, making them inoperable.

When Jesus and His disciples were on their way to Jerusalem for the last time, Jesus explained to them what was about to happen. " 'Behold, we are going up to Jerusalem, and the Son of Man will be betrayed to the chief priests and to the scribes; and they will condemn Him to death and deliver Him to the Gentiles; and they will mock Him, and scourge Him, and spit on Him, and kill Him. And the third day He will rise again' " (Mark 10:33, 34).

There was stunned silence for a while as these words of doom settled down upon the group. It seemed each disciple was grappling with the thought, trying to make sense of it. Surely, one of them would come up with some words of encouragement for the sorrowing Jesus. "Then James and John, the sons of Zebedee, came to Him, saying, 'Teacher, we want You to do for us whatever we ask.' And He said to them, 'What do you want Me to do for you?' They said to Him, 'Grant us that we may sit, one on Your right hand and the other on Your left, in Your glory' " (Mark 10:35–37).

Incredible! What a blow to the heart of the Savior! If it weren't recorded in the Bible, it would be unbelievable. It was if they were saying, "Oh, really? That's nice, but could You do us a favor?" Apparently, they hadn't heard a word He had said. If they had heard, they weren't thinking of Him and His sorrow; they were thinking of what would happen to them. After three years of patient training, they still believed that Jesus was going to set up an earthly kingdom, and they wanted to make their positions the highest possible. As usual, they were thinking about themselves.

What James and John did would be like the following interchange. You: "Pastor, I just found out that I have a serious problem. Next week I must have a surgery that will last hours. Sometimes patients don't survive. Pastor, I'm so worried." Me: "That's nice. Say, I want to take my wife out to a nice restaurant tonight. Could you loan me fifty dollars?"

A person could say the brothers were simply by faith looking past Christ's suffering to His future glory. That may be, but it seems to me more likely that their request was an evidence of their insensitivity to what Jesus had just said and a testimony to the lengths proud people will go to put themselves at the head of the line.

WHO'S THE GREATEST?

This wasn't the first time the disciples had stumbled on the question of who would get the most prestigious positions in the kingdom of heaven. Sometime earlier, they had asked, "Who then is the greatest in the kingdom of heaven?"

Jesus answered by calling a little child to Him, setting the child in the midst of them, and saying, " 'Unless you are converted and become as little children, you will by no means enter the kingdom of heaven. Therefore whoever humbles himself as this little child is the greatest in the kingdom of heaven' " (Matthew 18:3, 4).

Humble one's self as a little child? Surely this doesn't mean kicking and screaming when we don't get our way, or fighting with our brothers and sisters. We already do those things; that's not a new concept. No, Jesus wasn't saying that we should *do* what children do but that we should *be* like children. They're dependent for their very existence on their parents. So, putting self aside, we should be dependent on our heavenly Father for all that we are. But while children will eventually grow up and no longer need their parents to care for them, we will need Jesus as much thirty years from now as we did the first day we gave our lives to Him.

One day Jesus told a parable about a Pharisee and a tax collector.

> He spoke this parable to some who trusted in themselves that they were righteous, and despised others: "Two men went up to the temple to pray, one a Pharisee and the other a tax collector. The Pharisee stood and prayed thus with himself, 'God, I thank You that I am not like other men—extortioners, unjust, adulterers, or even as this tax collector. I fast twice a week; I give tithes of all that I possess.'
>
> "And the tax collector, standing afar off, would not so much as raise his eyes to heaven, but beat his breast, saying, 'God, be merciful to me a sinner!'
>
> "I tell you, this man went down to his house justified rather than the other; for everyone who exalts himself will be humbled, and he who humbles himself will be exalted" (Luke 18:9–14).

The people who were listening to the story may well have seen something like this happen in real time. The words of the Pharisee were what some would call "positive self-talk." What he meant was, "God, look at me. I've arrived. I won't be needing You anymore."

When Jesus said, " 'Blessed are the meek, / For they shall inherit the earth' " (Matthew 5:5), He was talking about a person's relationship with God. The meek never stop recognizing their dependence on God. On the other hand, the proud figure they are past that stage.

Have you ever looked into the "self-esteem" movement? The premise is that we can't love God or our neighbor until we love ourselves. Self-esteem creates a new order of relationship that puts me first, God second, and everyone else third. This philosophy effectively leaves mute the subject of meekness and humility because it ignores our Lord's command to seek first the kingdom of God and His righteousness. Second, it makes of none effect Philippians 2:3: "Let nothing be done through selfish ambition or conceit, but *in lowliness of mind let each esteem others better than himself*" (emphasis added). The focus on *I*, *me*, and *mine* is not only influencing the home but the church as well.

In his famous inaugural speech in 1961, John F. Kennedy challenged the nation: "Ask not what your country can do for you; ask what you can do for your country." We used to come to church to worship God and learn how to serve Him. Now it's as if the call were, "Ask not what I can do for the church, but ask what the church can do for me."

It's not uncommon to hear people say that they're looking for a church that meets their needs. As a result, many churches seem to be turning their focus away from God and His glory and are focusing their attention on what the business world calls the "consumer." We now hear talk about how to "market" the gospel in order to attract people. Worship services are increasingly focused on attracting a certain market group, be they the youth, the newly married, the seniors, or somewhere in between. The aim is to please the worshiper rather than the One who is being worshiped.

The contemporary culture is at loggerheads with all that the kingdom of God stands for. To many, Jesus has become only an icon. His teachings, though admittedly devotional, are considered outdated and unrealistic—meant for another time and place. " 'He that humbles himself shall be exalted'? You've got to be kidding! If you don't exalt yourself, nobody else will. How can you ever get ahead if you're humble?" And to show its contempt for the very idea of humility, the world has invented a humbley, bumbley character named Walter Mitty. According to the encyclopedia, "Mitty is a meek, mild man with a vivid fantasy life. The character's name has come into more general use to refer to an ineffectual dreamer." This is the idea that the devil wants you to have of humility.

ANTIDOTE FOR STRESS

By contrast, the Holy Spirit's fruit of true humility is an answer to one of the most pervasive problems of humankind today. Who hasn't heard of stress? Who hasn't been stressed out at one time or another? Jesus offers the antidote for stress. You'll find it in, of all places, meekness and humility. You may not have seen it this way before, but notice His words: " 'Come to Me, all you who labor and are heavy laden, and I will give you rest. Take My yoke upon you and learn from Me, for I am gentle and lowly in heart, and you will find rest for your souls. For My yoke is easy and My burden is light' " (Matthew 11:28–30).

How is this an antidote for stress? Yokes ease the carrying of burdens. Each of us has burdens, and they're all different. But there's one burden we share alike, and that is life itself. The question is not if we will carry burdens. Jesus did. He was despised and rejected, a Man of sorrows and acquainted with grief. The question is how we will carry them.

What does Jesus say about how we can carry our burdens?

He says, "Learn of Me."

Learn what?

Learn that "I am meek and lowly."

Meekness may not make the problems of life go way, but it will make them bearable.

In the time of Jesus, it wasn't only oxen that bore yokes. People placed yokes across their shoulders to carry heavy loads. Jesus was a carpenter. He knew a good yoke from a bad one. He knew which ones pinched and which ones fit and made the load easier to bear. His yoke—that is, His way of carrying the burden of life—is meekness and humility. With these qualities of the Spirit, the burdens in our lives will be easier to bear.

A meek and quiet spirit doesn't look out for itself but derives true satisfaction from serving others. Meekness and humility keep life's burdens on the outside so that we don't internalize them. Our burdens are not us, and we are not our burdens. We may suffer hard knocks, but they can't damage our heart or mind, where we really live, because it's who we are that counts.

"Meekness is a precious grace, willing to suffer silently, willing to endure trials. Meekness is patient and labors to be happy under all circumstances. Meekness is always thankful and makes its own songs of happiness, making melody in the heart of God. Meekness will suffer disappointment and wrong and will not retaliate."[1]

Those of us who have participated in the ordinance of humility all our lives may think little of the ceremony while we're participating in it. Often we engage in light banter. We pour the water, dry the basin, and put the used towel in the basket all without thinking. We thank the other person, perhaps have a quick prayer with them, and return to the sanctuary for the Lord's Supper.

In the time of Jesus, it was considered necessary for someone to wash the feet of guests when they came to visit. You can image that, in an environment where most people wore sandals, washing one's feet was more than a courtesy. But the hosts never did it themselves; it was always done by a servant. The servants who washed the feet of others were considered, as we would say, to be low on society's totem pole.

When the disciples gathered in the upper room, they had made no provision for a servant. As the story goes, Jesus "rose from supper and laid aside His garments, took a towel and girded Himself. After that, He poured water into a basin and began to wash the disciples' feet, and to wipe them with the towel with which He was girded" (John 13:4, 5).

That Jesus should wash their feet was unthinkable. This is why Peter said, "Don't touch me!" In other words, "I won't let You lower Yourself to the role of a servant."

A few minutes later, Jesus said, " 'You call Me Teacher and Lord, and you say well, for so I am. If I then, your Lord and Teacher, have washed your feet, you also ought to wash one another's feet. For I have given you an example, that you should do as I have done to you' " (John 13:13–15).

Jesus wasn't role-playing when He washed the disciples' feet that night so long ago. When He said He had given them an example, He wasn't talking about cleanliness but about being humble. The disciples had just been talking among themselves about who would be the greatest in the kingdom, and this was Jesus' lesson for them. It wasn't simply to initiate a ritual that we now perform four times a year; it was all about humility. That's the importance Jesus attributes to this fruit of the Spirit.

"Let this mind be in you which was also in Christ Jesus, who, being in the form of God, did not consider it robbery to be equal with God, but made Himself of no reputation, taking the form of a bondservant, and coming in the likeness of men. And being found in appearance as a man, He humbled Himself and became obedient to the point of death, even the death of the cross" (Philippians 2:5–8).

> Must Jesus bear the cross alone,
> And all the world go free?
> No, there's a cross for everyone,
> And there's a cross for me.
> —Thomas Shepherd

Being like Jesus is like attempting to climb a mountain so high that no one can climb it alone. We can't be humble, meek, and lowly unless we receive these qualities as fruit of the Spirit. Even as we cultivate these gifts, we'll never be able to say, "Have you noticed how humble I am?" If we did so, we would be like the man who wrote the book *Humility and How I Obtained It.*

There's a story of two ducks and a frog that lived happily together in a farm pond. The best of friends, the three would play together at their waterhole. When the hot summer days came, however, the pond began to dry up, and soon it was evident they would have to move. This was no problem for the ducks, which could fly to another pond. But the frog couldn't move away as easily. So the frog got a stick and suggested that each duck grab an end in its bill, and he would hang on to the middle with his mouth as they flew to another pond.

The plan worked well—so well, in fact, that as they were flying along, a farmer looked up in admiration and mused, "Well, isn't that a clever idea! I wonder who thought of that?" Whereupon the proud frog spoke his last words: "I did!"

That story reminds me of the text, "Pride goes before destruction, / And a haughty spirit before a fall" (Proverbs 16:18). In our hearts, in our homes, and in the church, we need to remind ourselves often of the words of our Lord, "I am meek and lowly of heart."

Meekness is not doing. Meekness is being.

---

1. White, *My Life Today,* 56.

THINKING IT OVER

1. List several ways meekness would change the environment of your home.
2. Think of three people you know who are humble. How do you recognize their humility?
3. Consider seriously whether you are willing for the Holy Spirit to give you the fruit of meekness.

CHAPTER 10

HOW TO BECOME STRONG WITHOUT LIFTING WEIGHTS

Giving all diligence, add to your faith . . . self-control.
—*2 Peter 1:5, 6*

The last fruit mentioned in the list of the fruits of the Spirit given in Galatians 5 is self-control. In your Bible, you may see the word *temperance* instead. That's because the words mean the same thing. Which one you see depends on which Bible translation you're using.

Have you ever wondered why self-control is mentioned last in this list? Well, one of the fruits has to be last. I guess the issue is whether there's any significance that we should consider to which one is last in the list.

It may be that self-control is mentioned last because it's the most important spiritual gift of all. I say that because self-control is the foundation of all the fruit of the Spirit and makes the other fruit possible. Using computer terminology, the Holy Spirit uses self-control to boot up the other fruit of the Spirit. Without self-control, sooner or later, the Christian's life would crash. I believe that as you read this chapter, you'll understand why this is so.

When we hear the term *self-control,* we usually think of food and sexual drives. And no wonder, because every day, everywhere, and in every way, we're being tempted in these areas. Madison Avenue uses sex to sell everything. So when sex is used to sell food—as it often is— our appetites can go out of control.

There has been much in the news lately about how people of today are becoming fatter than the previous generation. Much of the blame is placed on fast food and the lack of exercise. Is that all there is to self-control? Just because we might be an ideal weight, we mustn't think we're better than our corpulent neighbors. A friend of mine, who, by his own admission, is overweight, once said to me, "The difference between me and some others I know is that my weakness is visible on the outside."

It's interesting how quick we are to notice someone who is overweight. But there's another side to the coin when it comes to identifying a glutton. You may associate the word *glutton* with excess weight. Actually, the word means "a food lover." So, gluttons may be fat, but they also may be thin. There are people who think of nothing but food—that is, they're obsessed with their diet; their lives revolve around eating, albeit eating the right things. For them, what a person eats has become the gold standard of the Christian life. They're hard on themselves and therefore hard on others.

I was once at a church retreat, minding my own business, when a person approached me and asked if I wanted to be a member of the 144,000. Well, you can't say No to that question; but when you say Yes, you have to beware of what's coming next. In this case, that person shoved a book in front of me and pointed to the "translation diet." If only translation were a matter of diet!

If it's not too much of something, it's too little of something else. There are those who worry so much about whether or not they drink eight glasses of water on Sabbath that they will pull out their water bottle while seated in the pew during the worship service.

Maybe the key word here is *obsessed*. A person who is obsessed with food may be so focused on where their next tossed salad is coming from that they short out the Lord's command to love their neighbor as themselves. You know how it's so easy for us to think unkindly of those who don't eat the way we do.

MY OBSESSIONS

Speaking of obsessions, unless I'm intentional, I tend to be obsessive myself. If you had visited my office a few years ago, you would have seen one of the most beautiful displays of African violets ever. And at home, my backyard had dozens of orchids hanging here and there. My tendency has always been to overdo a good thing. It sounds ridiculous, but sometimes I would get an insatiable urge to buy a new orchid plant—which meant a fifty-mile trip to an orchid barn and fifty miles back. And—*Voilà!*—forty dollars later, there was yet another orchid hanging in my backyard.

If you had seen my flowers without hearing of my excesses, you would probably have congratulated me for my wholesome hobby. But looking back, I can see it was a hobby gone wild. It had become an obsession—too much of a good thing.

Is it possible to get too much of a good thing? I would have to say Yes. It's a matter of self-control.

The Lord is not against eating but against gluttony. He loves flowers. After all, He made them. But He would warn about excess. The Lord isn't against sex either, but He is against lust and an obsession with sex. Notice the works of the flesh that precede the list of the fruit of the Spirit: "The works of the flesh are evident, which are: adultery, fornication, uncleanness, lewdness, idolatry, sorcery, hatred, contentions, jealousies, outbursts of wrath, selfish ambitions, dissensions, heresies, envy, murders, drunkenness, revelries, and the like; of which I tell you beforehand, just as I also told you in time past, that those who practice such things will not inherit the kingdom of God" (Galatians 5:19–21). While there can be too much of a good thing, there is also that which is expressly forbidden. Inasmuch as we are surrounded with sensual suggestions, a lack of self-control in these areas will spell failure.

The very air we breathe is full of temptations for moral impurity— from sexual addictions to pornography on the Internet; from provocative fashions to the growing approval of homosexuality. People don't need to do anything to get themselves wet in a hard rain. It's keeping dry that requires effort. And so it is with moral purity.

Jesus illustrated the seriousness of allowing oneself to be overtaken by the "works of the flesh" when He said, " 'If your hand or foot causes you to sin, cut it off and cast it from you. It is better for you to enter into life lame or maimed, rather than having two hands or two feet, to be cast into the everlasting fire. And if your eye causes you to sin, pluck it out and cast it from you. It is better for you to enter into life with one eye, rather than having two eyes, to be cast into hell fire' " (Matthew 18:8, 9).

History tells us that Origen, one of the church fathers of the second century, had himself castrated. His motive, of course, was that he believed that the sexual problem is a matter of anatomy. Scripture sees it differently: "Keep your heart with all diligence, / For out of it spring the issues of life" (Proverbs 4:23). We are not slaves to our organs, but rather our organs are slaves to us and do our bidding. This is why there's hope for us in the gift of self-control.

The person who has trouble with food is the one who thinks about it all the time. The person who has trouble with sex and lust is the one who thinks about them all the time. Our problems are not the stomach or the sex organs; they're problems of the mind. That's why Scripture teaches that out of the heart are the issues of life. That's why Jesus will daily give us a new heart if we will ask.

Jesus said, " 'Those who are well have no need of a physician, but those who are sick' " (Mark 2:17). And, of course, ministers aren't supposed to get sick spiritually, never mind the fact that we're human. But we can easily fall into one of two ditches. Either we can tell people what's wrong with them, or we can tell them everything is OK when it really isn't. But can we recognize and admit that sometimes we ourselves need help?

Some years ago, I was convicted that I needed to ask the Lord for the fruit of self-control in my own life. It's one thing to preach what others need; it's another thing to admit one's own problems and shortcomings. But I had come to that point, so I began to pray for self-control.

You won't believe what happened! Did I stop growing African violets? Did I quit buying orchids? No, none of that. I had settled those obvious things long before. But I began to notice changes in other completely unrelated areas of my life. I started hanging up my clothes instead of just throwing them on the bed after work. I began to keep my side of the closet neat. I cleaned out the garage, finding a place for everything and putting everything in its place. And during that same period, I lost twenty pounds! Those were out-of-control areas of my life that I hadn't even noticed. But evidently God had, being the God of order that He is.

THE FIRE-STARTER

While it's comparatively easy to talk to young people about their proclivity to immorality and to those who are overweight about the advantages of the vegan diet, it's much more difficult to admit the big sins in our own lives. What about the lack of self-control in the way we often talk to each other? Maybe I should have said, talk *at* each other.

Please read what follows prayerfully.

If anyone does not stumble in word, he is a perfect man,

able also to bridle the whole body. Indeed, we put bits in horses' mouths that they may obey us, and we turn their whole body. Look also at ships: although they are so large and are driven by fierce winds, they are turned by a very small rudder wherever the pilot desires.

Even so the tongue is a little member and boasts great things. See how great a forest a little fire kindles! And the tongue is a fire, a world of iniquity. The tongue is so set among our members that it defiles the whole body, and sets on fire the course of nature; and it is set on fire by hell.

For every kind of beast and bird, of reptile and creature of the sea, is tamed and has been tamed by mankind. But no man can tame the tongue. It is an unruly evil, full of deadly poison. With it we bless our God and Father, and with it we curse men, who have been made in the similitude of God. Out of the same mouth proceed blessing and cursing. My brethren, these things ought not to be so.

Does a spring send forth fresh water and bitter from the same opening? Can a fig tree, my brethren, bear olives, or a grapevine bear figs? Thus no spring yields both salt water and fresh.

Who is wise and understanding among you? Let him show by good conduct that his works are done in the meekness of wisdom. But if you have bitter envy and self-seeking in your hearts, do not boast and lie against the truth. This wisdom does not descend from above, but is earthly, sensual, demonic (James 3:2–15).

That's quite a discourse on self-control, isn't it? And so up to the minute, it could have been written yesterday. James distills his sermon into just one sentence: "So then, my beloved brethren, let every man be swift to hear, slow to speak, slow to wrath; for the wrath of man does not produce the righteousness of God" (James 1:19, 20).

There may be a few times when you wish you had said something, but there's a world of grief in wishing you hadn't said something in haste. Once something is spoken, it's impossible to take it back. We don't always have to have the last word.

What's the point? "There's a wonderful power in silence. When impatient words are spoken to you, do not retaliate. Words spoken in reply to one who is angry usually act as a whip, lashing the temper into greater fury. But anger met by silence quickly dies away. Let the Christian bridle his tongue, firmly resolving not to speak harsh, impatient words. With the tongue bridled, he may be victorious in every trial of patience through which he is called to pass."[1]

Sometimes when I'm giving seminars on marriage, I use the following ridiculous illustration. Suppose my wife, Betty, comes home from running some errands. When she enters the house, she sees me sitting on the sofa in the family room and says, "Oh, there you are again, ugly. What a jerk! I wish I had never married you." (Forgive me, Betty; this is only a bad illustration!) I'm sure you would agree with me that these are terrible words—fighting words! But let me point out that there'll be no fight without my participation. How I respond is key to what happens next. Self-control—do you see? If I ignore those terrible words, they'll just fly off into space. But if I come back with equally harsh words, who knows where the story will end and what damage will be done?

The tongue that is not under the power of the Holy Spirit is a fire that is indeed earthly, sensual, and devilish. The result is mental and physical abuse, broken homes, and scarred lives. And because the church is comprised of homes, it, too, is seriously affected by an uncontrolled tongue.

FINDING THE POWER

Chapter 7 of the book of Romans is at the heart of the subject of self-control. Often, people will discuss whether Romans 7 was Paul's testimony before he was converted or afterward. I believe this is his testimony after he met the Lord. The point he's making here is that although he has the desire to do the will of God, he doesn't have the power. If I were asked if I have the willpower not to do this or that, the answer according to Romans 7 and 8 is that I may have the will but not the power. The fact is that before we come to Jesus, we're practicing sinners. When we come to Jesus, we receive a new heart; but—using an illustration from the world of computer science again—the old nature, while overwritten, still remains. This is why the apostle Paul writes, "I discipline my body and bring it into subjection, lest, when I have preached to others, I myself should become disqualified" (1 Corinthians 9:27).

We can't ask that the Holy Spirit control us. God won't control us. He designed that we be free moral agents. Full of the Spirit, yes; controlled by the Spirit, no. While the devil takes our wills captive, the gospel gives our wills back to us.

My will is me. It's the essence of who I am. I can't give God my will, but I can will—choose—to do His will. In the Garden of Gethsemane, Jesus declared that His will was to do His Father's will.

> No outward observances can take the place of simple faith and entire renunciation of self. But no man can empty himself of self. We can only consent for Christ to accomplish the work. Then the language of the soul will be, Lord, take my heart; for I cannot give it. It is Thy property. Keep it pure, for I cannot keep it for Thee. Save me in spite of myself, my weak, unchrist-like self. Mold me, fashion me, raise me into a pure and holy atmosphere, where the rich current of Thy love can flow through my soul.[2]

THE FRUIT OF THE SPIRIT

Many have thought that giving their lives to Jesus would mean that temptation would end. When they discover otherwise, they conclude that they must not have been sincere and there's no hope for them. The difference between our lives before Christ and afterward is that before Christ we were slaves to sin. We may have wished to be free but had no power to free ourselves. When our will is combined with Christ's will, in Him we have the power to be free from sin. But we must continue to choose to serve Him every day. If we don't continually make this decision, little by little, we'll find ourselves going backward until once more we become slaves to sin.

The fruit of self-control is that part of me that says Yes to what the Holy Spirit wants to do in my life. When we have the fruit of self-control, victory over sin becomes a reality and we experience the sweetness of the rest of the fruit of the Spirit.

Who is in control of my life? I am. Otherwise, why is it called self-control? Who gives me victory over the sins that so easily beset me? It's the Holy Spirit. "I can do all things through Christ who strengthens me" (Philippians 4:13).

In the Christian life, self-control doesn't take us out of the battle, but it puts us on the winning side. Remember the old saying, "When in doubt, read the directions"? God's Word is our directions. David wrote, "Your word is a lamp to my feet / And a light to my path" (Psalm 119:105). Would someone please turn on the light!

---

1. Ellen G. White, *Reflecting Christ* (Hagerstown, Md.: Review and Herald®, 1985), 293.

2. White, *Christ's Object Lessons* (Mountain View, Calif.: Pacific Press®, 1941), 159.

Thinking It Over

1. Identify the things in your life that you have to admit are obsessions, be their objects good or bad.
2. How have your obsessions affected your life? How have they affected the lives of those around you?
3. If someone were to ask you to tell them in plain, easy-to-understand language how to get victory over bad habits, what would you say?

CHAPTER 11

PUTTING IT INTO PRACTICE

Stand therefore, . . . having put on the breastplate of righteousness.
—Ephesians 6:14

There's no such thing as a theoretical Christian. While the fruit of the Spirit considered thus far has to do with attitudes, righteousness makes practical applications of these attitudes in the Christian life. *Righteous,* then, describes the life of a person who is putting into practice the fruit of the Spirit.

We have no difficulty thinking of Jesus or even Noah as righteous, but when it comes to applying what it means to be righteous to our own life, we often fall into one of two errors. On one hand, we may think that because Jesus is righteous and salvation is by faith, we don't have to be concerned about the details of our lives. On the other hand, we may conclude that doing something good, like sweeping the floor, and not doing something bad, like not robbing a bank, in and of themselves comprise righteousness. I heard of a leader of a Bible study group who fell to the second error. This man was earnest and very conscientious. After a moving presentation on the nearness of the coming of

Christ, he, in all sincerity, concluded the study by saying, "We know Jesus is about to return, so why are we still drinking Coke?"

According to Scripture, righteousness is the test of those who have been born again. "If you know that He is righteous, you know that everyone who practices righteousness is born of Him" (1 John 2:29). "Little children, let no one deceive you. He who practices righteousness is righteous, just as He is righteous" (1 John 3:7).

But Paul raises a dilemma for us. He wrote, quoting from the Old Testament, that there is "none righteous, no, not one" (Romans 3:10). How can the born-again Christian be righteous if no one is righteous?

The answer is that righteousness is not something we do or even something that we naturally are. Righteousness is a gift of the Holy Spirit. "If by the one man's offense death reigned through the one, much more those who receive abundance of grace and of the gift of righteousness will reign in life through the One, Jesus Christ" (Romans 5:17). This gift is like a robe that Jesus puts over our shoulders when we confess our sins. It covers our own stained and torn clothes so that we become part of God's family. This is called imputed righteousness.

But this robe does something more. Since our stained and torn clothes are covered with this robe and we have become part of God's family, we now want to behave like God's children. We recognize that we are different now; we've become new people. This is called imparted righteousness. It's the same robe of righteousness given to us by Jesus, yet it does these two things for us.

Imputed righteousness has to do with how we are saved. We're saved because Jesus bought us back with His life. Imparted righteousness has to do with what the robe of Jesus' righteousness does for us.

How does this robe of righteousness change us? Does it change just the way we look? And why were our clothes stained and torn before? What happened to us?

The Bible gives the answer in one beautiful verse: "As by one man's disobedience many were made sinners, so also by one Man's obedience many will be made righteous" (Romans 5:19). Our lives were stained and torn by our disobedience, but Jesus covers us with His righteous life (the "new clothes") in order to restore us to obedience.

Someone may ask, "What does obedience have to do with being righteous?" The answer is "Everything"; because a person who lives a righteous life will be obedient, and a person who lives an obedient life will be living a righteous life. Simply stated, the righteous are obedient.

Obedience didn't put Lucifer into heaven, but his disobedience did take him out. In the same way, Adam and Eve were not put into the Garden of Eden because of their obedience, but they *were* expelled because of their disobedience.

Righteousness and obedience are linked together and cannot be separated. We cannot appreciate the gift of righteousness until we understand the significance of obedience. For this reason, this chapter on the fruit of righteousness will focus on the meaning of obedience.

OBEDIENCE AND RIGHTEOUSNESS

The obedience that is an integral component of righteousness isn't self-generated. People who aren't converted can't obey God, because the carnal heart isn't subject to the law of God (Romans 8:7). People who have received salvation by faith in Jesus will be obedient. Obedience is the objective test as to whether a person has received salvation or not.

True obedience has five important characteristics.

1. True obedience is based on an attitude of the heart. First and foremost, obedience comes from the heart. It's a purpose and a desire of the heart. Obedience must begin in the heart because people can appear to be obedient but hate every minute of the charade.

A problem many have in respect to obedience is the impression that obedience is somehow our part in salvation. Some have thought that salvation has two parts—God's part and our part. However, the fact is that salvation is all God's doing. He not only forgives our sins, but also, in a miraculous way, gives us—if we will accept it—the attitude of actually wanting to obey Him, to do whatever He asks. The primary purpose of salvation is to create in us new hearts—that is, a new attitude that says, "I delight to do Your will, O my God. You have written Your commandments in my heart." To hunger and thirst after righteousness (Matthew 5:6) means to long to do the will of God. In short then, wanting to be obedient and wanting to do the will of God are the same thing.

Jesus said, " 'He who has My commandments and keeps them, it is he who loves Me. And he who loves Me will be loved by My Father, and I will love him and manifest Myself to him' " (John 14:21). He also said, " 'If anyone loves Me, he will keep My word' " (John 14:23). I'm thrilled as I realize that day by day Jesus is giving me a heart that loves to obey.

A new attitude is necessary, however, because people persuaded against their will are always of the same opinion still. People who don't have an attitude of obedience will tend to play obedience games. That is, they'll be obedient in some things and disobedient in others. But true obedience is nondiscriminatory. It's motivated by an attitude that operates all the time. Some people obey some of God's commandments and knowingly disobey others. They're not 50 percent obedient or almost obedient; they're simply disobedient.

A person who is righteous in the eyes of God desires to obey what God requires. So the first characteristic of true obedience is that it is a desire—an attitude—that God puts in our hearts.

2. God calculates a person's obedience in view of that person's capacity to obey. Obedience becomes a desire of the heart when people accept Jesus as their Savior and the process of salvation begins to influence their life. But this doesn't mean that they will always obey God perfectly. We must not confuse a life of obedience with absolute perfection.

Although God uses the same yardstick on all of us, He doesn't hold us all equally accountable. He considers where a person comes from, that person's background, and what opportunities he or she has had. This may not be fair, but it's just. Fairness says that if you have a dollar and there are four people, each one gets a quarter. Fairness gives to each person equally. But God acts from the principle of justice. Justice divides the dollar according to the greatest need.

To apply the standard by which a first-grader gets A's to a person studying for a PhD would be absurd. In the same way, the standard that applies to a PhD candidate would completely crush a first-grader. A first-grader goes to school with a desire to learn. He makes mistakes along the way, but his attitude to learn makes it possible for him to grow. In the Christian life, it's a little like going to school. Along the way, we will make mistakes; but we will have an obedient attitude that will acknowledge the mistakes and enable us to learn from them.

It will help us to understand if we see obedience from God's point of view. The apostle James writes, "To him who knows to do good and does not do it, to him it is sin" (James 4:17). In other words, God holds people accountable for the light they have. A child of five can be as obedient as a youth of twenty-two; the difference between the two lies in what's expected of each one.

Good students try to get 100 percent on their examinations. When they miss a question, they're not satisfied. Recognizing their weakness in that area, they'll give special attention to the subject until they're able to get the answer right the next time.

Two giants of faith and righteousness, Noah and Abraham, weren't perfect. Genesis 9:21 reveals that Noah got drunk. Yet those whom God has accounted as righteous have always been men and women who had a deep, heartfelt commitment to Him.

3. Obedience is about voluntary sin. We can clarify our picture of obedience if we can see the difference between voluntary and involuntary sin. When God talks about disobedience, He's talking about voluntary sin—that is, sinning with impunity. There's an important difference between a student who tries to make a good grade on an exam but misses a few points and a student who says he doesn't care and is just trying to get by. Similarly, there's an enormous difference between the person who prays every day to be obedient and the person who believes that obedience is unimportant or unattainable.

Obedient Christians are always sensitive to their failures and mistakes, and by prayer and the engrafting of the Word of God by the Holy Spirit, they're ever pressing on toward the mark of the high calling of God in Christ Jesus.

By now you may be thinking, *But Pastor O'Ffill, you make it sound as though obedience were a relative word.* Well, in a way it is. But no one from any generation will be saved who in his heart of hearts is knowingly and willfully disobedient to the Lord. Likewise, everyone in every generation who is fully committed to the Lord is filled with a heartfelt desire to please and obey Him.

4. Temptation is not disobedience. Here's some good news: temptation is not disobedience. Our nature and the devil continually call us to pride, impurity, and unholiness. No, the righteous are not those who have never been tempted. Often we think that because we are tempted, we are beyond redemption and not worth saving. The truth is that all great men and women of God were and are tempted. Jesus Himself was tempted. That's the work of the devil and his imps. They're busy 24/7 trying to lure God's people into sin. There's nothing wrong with us if—better, *when*—we're tempted. It's not temptation that is sin; it's giving in to temptation.

5. True obedience is never motivated by fear, guilt, or duty. The righteous don't obey God for fear of the consequences. Scripture says that perfect love casts out fear (1 John 4:18). Those who obey out of fear of the consequences are slaves and not sons. Those who obey God because they're afraid not to don't know the meaning of the gift of righteousness. There are millions who believe that God is ready to strike them with some calamity if they aren't pious enough. Satan is the one who originated and promotes this misunderstanding. Jesus' life demonstrates how wrong this thinking is.

Guilt and dutifulness are just as faulty motivators for obedience as is fear. Some people try to obey God because they would feel guilty if they didn't. They're not the ones who are hungering and thirsting after righteousness. Likewise, those who try to obey God in every particular because they feel it's their duty to do so are in a sense trying to live a righteous life by holding their breath.

People who live under grace obey from a thankful heart. Living under the law—fearing every minute some terrible judgment—is not our heritage as sons and daughters of God. True obedience is heart deep; false obedience is only skin deep. When people hunger and thirst after righteousness, they will delight in keeping the commandments.

But beware: if you promote the keeping of the commandments these days, you may be labeled a legalist. And for many people, that label will immediately discredit what you say. It has become the ultimate insult. But rest assured—a legalist is not a person who wants to *keep* the commandments, but one who wants to *do* them. The Ten Commandments tell people what to *do,* but only a spirit of obedience will help the righteous *keep* them from the heart.

THE FRUIT OF RIGHT LIVING

Five minutes of implicit obedience to God at any point will generate more fruits of right living in our lives than five years of theological or doctrinal discussion that end only in dillydallying with the truth. The focus of those who hunger and thirst after righteousness will be the same as was that of our Lord, who said, " 'My food is to do the will of

Him who sent Me, and to finish His work' " (John 4:34). " 'I have come down from heaven, not to do My own will, but the will of Him who sent Me' " (John 6:38).

There are some who say they want the will of God for their lives. Others even say they are doing God's will. But many reserve the right to decide for themselves what God's will is. Some claim they're praying that God will help them do His will, when actually they've decided for themselves which of God's commandments are important for them. In reality, they're doing their own will rather than what God asks them to do. This attitude is evidenced in the person who runs off with someone else's wife and explains, "My God wants me to be happy."

The righteous ones are those who settle into the truth so that they cannot be moved. Like those who have gone before who through faith "subdued kingdoms, worked righteousness, obtained promises, [and] stopped the mouths of lions" (Hebrews 11:33), they will come behind in no good gift. The fruit of the Spirit that is righteousness will fit them to stand when there is " 'a time of trouble, / Such as never was since there was a nation' " (Daniel 12:1).

It's conceivable that a school teacher might give an exam on which no one could score 100 percent because the exam contained trick questions or questions that weren't covered in the course. But when it comes to righteousness, there are no trick questions nor questions not covered in the course. Paul's counsel to Timothy is for us as well: "Be diligent to present yourself approved to God, a worker who does not need to be ashamed, rightly dividing the word of truth" (2 Timothy 2:15). If a test is coming, we must study.

Study what? "You, O man of God [and woman of God], . . . pursue righteousness, godliness, faith, love, patience, gentleness" (1 Timothy 6:11). Hmmm . . . Those sound like the fruit of the Spirit, don't they?

In Ephesians 5:9, the apostle Paul lists three more dimensions of the fruit of the Spirit. They are goodness, righteousness, and truth. In the following two chapters, we will consider their role in the Spirit-filled life.

THINKING IT OVER

1. If someone were to ask you to explain to them the relationship between righteousness and obedience, what would you say?
2. What motives might people have for insisting that obedience is legalism—salvation by works? What are some characteristics of legalism?
3. Could people ever get to the place where they could call themselves righteous? Explain your answer.

CHAPTER 12

NOTHING BUT THE TRUTH

Stand therefore, having girded your waist with truth.
—Ephesians 6:14

I heard the neighbor children playing in their backyard. One of them began to chant, "Liar, liar, pants on fire!" A study on human behavior revealed that people tell as many as fifty lies a day. One of the most common lies is "The check is in the mail." Another is "I was only kidding." Here's a very common lie: "I'll get to it right away." Believe it or not, another popular lie is "I'm sorry," along with "I didn't mean to hurt your feelings." A lie used by many is "Oh no, you didn't wake me up."

She was where she shouldn't have been. She was alone, which she shouldn't have been. And then she saw something she needn't ever have seen—a talking snake. It wasn't like the snakes I sometimes find in my backyard here in Florida. This snake asked her a question—the same question that would continue to tickle the fancy of humankind down through the ages: "Wouldn't you like to be able to decide for yourself what's right and what's wrong?"

Her answer was cautious—not a Yes or a No, but rather an apology: "God has said that if we eat the fruit of this tree, we will die." The snake quickly returns with "No, you won't." (See Genesis 2:15–17; 3:1–3.)

Of course, it wasn't really a snake that was talking; it was the fallen angel who had been the covering cherub. The Bible tells us that Satan is the father of lies (John 8:44). To paraphrase, we could say that lies are the devil's native language. When we lie, we are, in effect, allowing ourselves to become puppets of the devil, and he becomes a ventriloquist.

Nowadays, we don't use the word *lie*—at least not as often as we used to. There are other, more acceptable words, like *cover-up* or *misleading,* or words that you hear in political circles: *misinformation* or *spin-doctoring.*

Lies affect the everyday lives of us all. A Christian repairman who works for a national repair franchise said that his boss gave him the order that when someone calls in requesting service, he was to say they would have someone out within two days, whether or not it was possible.

I was talking to a young man who worked at a large retail store. He confessed that he had been instructed never to say "I don't know." When I heard this, I thought of the times I had come into that tool department to ask the sales person which tool would be best for the job I was doing. Whoever was on duty would recommend this or that tool, and I'd buy it. Now here is this fellow telling me that, even though he may not have had a clue, he has to say something—and so he guesses.

Even those who claim to be Christians have become somewhat confused in this matter of telling the truth. But there I go, doing it like the rest. I shouldn't have said *confused,* because that's the excuse we give when we don't want to do what we know is right.

CONFUSED ABOUT THE TRUTH

A fellow explained to me his view of the commandment "Thou

shalt not bear false witness against thy neighbor." He said, "Notice that the commandment says, 'against thy neighbor.' The key word is *against.*" He went on to say that if it's for a person's good or for a greater good, it's all right to lie. According to his interpretation, the commandment doesn't mean that you shouldn't tell an untruth; it just means don't do something that would hurt your neighbor. Now, that's what I call a broad interpretation. But there I go again. That isn't a broad interpretation; it's a wrong interpretation. Isn't there a text about "rightly dividing the word of truth" (2 Timothy 2:15)? When will we finally reject everything we know is wrong and call it by its right name?

The apostle John says that Jesus was full of grace and truth (John 1:14). And if we, as followers of Jesus, are under His grace, we, too, should be full of truth—and this doesn't mean just doctrinal truth.

A lie is a lie, but lies often come in a variety packages. For example, there's what is called a white lie. Most of us would agree that a bold-faced lie is in the big-league category and has no place in the Christian life. But many of us have participated in little white lies. For example, the phone rings and we don't want to talk with the caller, so we tell the person who answered the phone, "Tell them I'm not home." Or we'd rather take advantage of the beautiful weather than go to the office, so we call in sick. And the list goes on.

We consider these little white lies harmless—or at least a better alternative at the time than telling the truth. But the Bible doesn't classify lies by color. There's no such thing as a little white lie—or a big white lie, for that matter. Either a thing is true or it's a lie.

Another form of lying is flattery. Flattery is counterfeit caring. It means, "I'll tell you what you want to hear so I can get from you what I want to have." Take a moment and read Psalm 12:2. Notice how the words *flattery* and *double-minded* go together.

Then there's what is called a half-truth. A half-truth is a lie because, though the information it contains is true, it doesn't give the whole picture. To purposely tell the truth out of context is to tell a lie.

Those who manifest truth as a fruit of the Spirit will be truthful in every way. If we want to stand for the truth in the future, we have to be people who always tell the truth and who love to hear the truth now. And we must be on guard. Error often comes wrapped in a skin of truth, making it difficult to recognize.

As we have noted, the very first sin Adam and Eve committed was introduced with a lie (see Genesis 3:4). And just as the devil used lies to begin the great controversy, so he'll use them to drive the events at its end.

TO TELL THE TRUTH

It happened when I was in the first grade. I don't remember what I'd done, but I do remember my teacher calling me to her desk. She told me to go to the principal's office and tell him that I had been a bad boy. I left my desk and went out into the hall, where it occurred to me that I didn't need to go to the principal's office; I could just stand in the hall for a few minutes and then return to my classroom. This I did. When I returned to my room, I wasn't prepared for the question the teacher asked me: "What did the principal say?"

Taken by surprise, I replied, "He told me to be a good boy."

During recess, I didn't feel like playing with the other kids. I remember standing alone by the fence at the back of the schoolyard. When school was over, my teacher patted me on the head and said, "You didn't go to the principal's office, did you?"

"No," I confessed as tears rolled down my checks. I had lied to my teacher and was sure this would disappoint my mother too. She always told me, "Dickey, better to die than to tell a lie."

I wonder if mothers tell this ideal to their children anymore. It doesn't seem so, because honesty is on the decline these days. Many people who know better have allowed themselves to get into the habit of lying.

There are those who like to point to instances in Scripture where men and women considered to be pious told lies. Because the Bible doesn't specifically condemn these people, it's sometimes assumed that under certain circumstances God condones lying. Rahab the prostitute who lived in Jericho is a case in point. She told a lie to protect the two spies who came to her house (Joshua 2:4).

Some say the story about Rahab and the spies means that the Bible recommends situation ethics—it's all right to tell a lie to save a life. If that were true, then, in effect, we'd be playing off the Ten Commandments against each other. A woman could work as a prostitute to earn money to help cover the cost of an evangelistic meeting, or a man could rob a bank to provide financial resources for the needy.

The Scriptures are scrupulously honest. They tell the life stories, warts and all, of men and women who became heroes for the Lord. Just because a person became a Bible hero doesn't mean that everything he or she did along the way was to the glory of God or is a model for the Christian life.

I don't say this to diminish any Bible character. The point is, we'll continue in our sins and perish in our sins unless we become perfectly honest with God, with ourselves, and with others. John 8:32 says, " 'You shall know the truth, and the truth shall make you free.' " The implication of this text is that not only is there an objective truth, which is in Jesus Christ, but we ourselves must come to the place where we prefer the truth. Not only must we prefer to hear the truth, we must prefer to tell the truth. Scripture teaches that those who are lost will not only be those who are into telling lies but also those who love to hear lies told (Revelation 22:15).

Lying, in fact, is high in the hierarchy of sins because it's the umbrella under which we justify all the other sins that we habitually commit. Lying is fatal to spiritual growth because it blocks us from receiving the truth, and without the truth, we cannot be set free from sin. We cannot gain victory over any sin until we have gotten the victory over telling lies.

"He who covers his sins will not prosper, / But whoever confesses and forsakes them will have mercy" (Proverbs 28:13). As long as we try to hide our sins from others and from ourselves, we will not repent, and if we won't repent, we won't be able to find the mercy of the Lord.

TO KNOW THE TRUTH

My dad once said that we will all remember what we were doing when we heard that President Kennedy had been shot—that's true, at least, of all those who were born before November 1963. For the rest of you, the watershed event was the attack on the World Trade Center in New York. The date was September 11, 2001. Chances are that you remember exactly what you were doing when you heard the news. Since that day, *terrorism* has become a household word.

One thing is certain: if the right people had known about the attack in advance, it wouldn't have happened. Think of all the deceptions surrounding that event! The terrorists were not the tourists their passports said they were. They weren't regular passengers on the airplanes. They weren't going where their tickets indicated. Nothing about them was the truth. The point is that not knowing the truth can easily become a matter of life or death. Regarding spiritual things, Jesus said, " 'Do not fear those who kill the body but cannot kill the soul. But rather fear Him who is able to destroy both soul and body in hell' " (Matthew 10:28).

There are some who say it makes no difference what we believe as long as we believe in Jesus. We must be careful with this. Let me explain. Before Jesus came to the earth the first time, there were people who believed in and looked forward to the coming of the Messiah.

Among them there were two groups: there were those who believed that the Messiah would come as a conquering king to rule the earth, and there were those—and they were the minority—who were expecting Him to come as prophesied in Isaiah 53—One who would be despised and rejected of men, a Man of sorrows and acquainted with grief. It made no difference what a person believed about the Messiah five hundred years before He came. The important thing was that people who lived then were looking forward by faith to His coming. It made no difference one hundred years or even fifty years before He came. But what they believed about the Messiah made all the difference in the world when He actually came, because those whose doctrine of the Messiah wasn't correct crucified Him.

It's simply not true that it makes no difference what you believe as long as you believe. Not knowing the truth on 9/11 cost the lives of more than three thousand people. In these last days, the majority of God's people have false doctrines and false expectations concerning the final events and the great deception. God has entrusted truth for this time to Seventh-day Adventists. Unless we love that truth and share it with others, great numbers of sincere Christians will be deceived when the antichrist makes his final move to ensnare the world. Remember, it's the devil's game plan to deceive as many as possible. Deceit is the name of his game.

There are some who subscribe to the idea that believing something will make it so. That may make a nice song title, but it's not a very sound argument. During the Middle Ages, most people believed the earth was flat. But just because something has been taught for a thousand years doesn't make it true. People could believe as long and firmly as they wanted to that the earth is flat, but it isn't.

A number of years ago, there was a television program called *To Tell the Truth*. The basic premise was simple: Several contestants each claimed to be a certain person, usually someone who held an unusual occupation or who had done something noteworthy. A panel of four celebrities questioned the contestants in an attempt to identify who was genuine and who was bluffing. After all the celebrities had a turn at questioning the guests, they voted on who they thought was the real contestant. When the voting was completed, the moderator said the now-famous line: "Will the real _____ please stand up?" Then the person in question stood, and the other contestants revealed who they really were.

The game was a lot of fun until you thought about it carefully. It was based on the false claimants telling lies in an attempt to deceive the panel. The show was entertaining the thousands of us who were watching through the lies of the contestants. It was honoring those whose lies fooled the judges. It was conditioning people to deceive. Looking back on it, I wonder why we thought it was so entertaining. If we thought about how God feels about lying, I doubt we would have been amused. In the last days, knowing the truth and telling the truth is a life-and-death matter.

The fruit of the Spirit is the truth, the whole truth, and nothing but the truth. Those who are receiving the gift of truth will personally know Him who is the Way, the Truth, and the Life (John 14:6). Those who are receiving the fruit of truth will be truthful. When Jesus returns to cleanse the earth of sin and its consequences, the Holy City will be the place of safety for the redeemed. Revelation warns that "whoever loves and practices a lie" will be outside that city, along with "sorcerers and sexually immoral and murderers and idolaters" (Revelation 22:15). Notice that it says not only those who tell lies but those who love to hear them.

What the serpent said so long ago was and is a lie. There is no such thing as a white lie or a little lie or a belief that in a time of crisis it doesn't matter. Thank God that we know Him who is the Truth, because He has made us free.

THINKING IT OVER

1. Revelation 22:15 refers to those who not only tell lies but love to hear them told. What do you think are some of the lies that people like to hear?

2. Under what kinds of circumstances have you been tempted to lie? What is the secret of always being truthful?

3. Do you agree that there is a "present truth"? What makes it different from any other truth?

CHAPTER

PUTTING FIRST THINGS FIRST

"Seek first the kingdom of God and His righteousness."
—Matthew 6:33

Earlier in this book, I said that we had recently remodeled our living and dining rooms. I didn't share all the details. Let me begin by saying that I'm a do-it-yourselfer, and if I can't make a certain repair, I don't hesitate to ask my youngest son, who lives close by, to give me a hand.

We've lived in our home for twenty-five years, so some upgrading was called for. The plan was that my son would install the simulated wood floor—the kind that looks like wood but wears like iron. We would then put on new baseboards, and a fresh coat of paint would be the finishing touch.

To begin the process, we took out the dinner table and the china closet, and I began to take down the pictures on the walls. In the process, I discovered a series of little eaten-out trails all over the backing of a picture I had just removed. A close look at the wall revealed a series of tiny holes where the picture had hung. You guessed it—termites.

I immediately called our exterminating company. (It pays to have one when you live in Florida.) They came to the house and checked out the wall. Fortunately, they didn't find any current activity; the colony must have moved on to greener pastures—or tastier pictures. The exterminator drilled tiny holes along the baseboard and pumped poison into the space between the walls, just in case. End of problem.

Maybe I'm taking the long way around, but the point is that when we discovered the termite damage, the rest of our plans came to a screeching halt. When you discover that termites have been in your walls, you don't just cover the walls with another coat of paint. By now I hope you've noticed the similarity between the action we took when we found the termite damage and the title of this chapter, which is the last in the book.

Have you ever made a presentation to a group of teenagers? What a wonderful, challenging experience that is! A few years ago, I was conducting a Week of Prayer in a church and was invited to speak to the young people at a local day academy during the chapel hour. Speaking to teens is a real challenge. I wondered what I could talk about that would pique their interest. It's not always easy to hold the attention of young people when talking about spiritual things.

An idea came to me that I figured just might be the ticket; so when I stood up to talk, I announced that I was going to give them three short seminars. Inasmuch as business people spend large sums of money attending seminars where they learn how to make more money, I would give them a free seminar on how to lose money. They had never heard of such a thing, so I immediately had their attention. You might be interested in learning about this yourself. After all, you're never too old to learn a new trick.

I began my first seminar by pointing out that one way to lose money is to neglect it. Sooner or later, inflation will erode its value. Just put your money under your mattress, and next year it will be worth less. I once had a Peruvian banknote that had been worth thirty-seven thousand dollars just seven years before the money was devalued. However, by the time I obtained the banknote, it was worth only about three cents.

Another way to lose money is to abandon it—finders keepers, losers weepers. Just leave the money lying around, and pretty soon it will disappear.

A third way to lose money is simply to waste it. End of seminar one. All the while the teens had been listening closely.

Then I announced that my next free seminar would be on how to lose your girlfriend. Needless to say, everyone sat up in their seats to hear this one. You can lose your girlfriend, I told them, the same way you lose money: neglect her, abandon her, or be unfaithful to her. End of seminar two.

By now they were right with me and appeared anxious to hear what the next free seminar was about. The last seminar, I said, was about how to lose Jesus as a Friend. Of course, I listed the same ways as those that would lose your money or your girlfriend: neglect, abandonment, unfaithfulness. End of seminar three. The chapel hour was over, and I was pleased. The talk had gone well.

WHAT REALLY MATTERS

The following Sabbath as I walked into the lobby of the church, the leader of the youth department asked me if I would mind talking to the young people again. When I walked into the youth Sabbath School room, I asked them if they remembered me. "Yes," they replied, "you spoke at chapel last Monday." (Score one for me.)

"Do you remember what I talked to you about?"

"Yes," they replied, "you told us how to lose money." (Score two for me.)

"How's that?" I asked.

They responded, "You neglect it, you abandon it, or you waste it." (Score three for me. I was beginning to think I should have been in youth ministries!)

"What else did I talk about?"

"You told us how to lose a girlfriend." (Score four.)

"And how's that?"

"Same way." (Score five for me. I'm on a roll.)

"What else did I talk about?"

Silence in the room.

"Come on!" I pleaded. "That was the main point of my talk."

The silence continued until someone said, "We don't remember."

I've never forgotten my experience that day in the youth department. Maybe they didn't learn a lesson, but I did. When I talked about how to lose money or one's girlfriend, they remembered everything. But when I talked about Jesus, somehow, they remembered nothing. What I learned about human nature that day is that the things we remember are the things that are important to us—and too often we're interested in anything or everything but the things that really matter.

Studying the fruit of the Spirit has been a life-changing experience for me. It's a thrill to know that it's not who I am (my profession, my degrees, my bank account, my clothes) but what I am (my character) that counts with Jesus. Jesus in my heart means the fruit of the Spirit in my life. I've realized that to have the fruit of the Spirit, I must put first things first. Receiving the fruit of the Spirit is not like typing in a URL and hitting Enter. There are steps to follow. These steps are not self-generated; rather, they're the result of responding to the Spirit. As we learned in the chapter on self-control, receiving the fruit of the Spirit is a *choice* we make. "It is God who works in you both to will and to do for His good pleasure" (Philippians 2:13). " 'Choose for yourselves this day whom you will serve. . . . But as for me and my house, we will serve the LORD' " (Joshua 24:15).

In order to receive the fruit of the Spirit, we must first repent. John the Baptist called those who came to him to repent and be baptized. "In those days John the Baptist came preaching in the wilderness of Judea, and saying, 'Repent, for the kingdom of heaven is at hand!' " (Matthew 3:1, 2).

Jesus began His ministry with the same call: "Jesus began to preach and to say, 'Repent, for the kingdom of heaven is at hand' " (Matthew 4:17). Often we speak of the need to return to Pentecost. To return to Pentecost is to repent. At the first Pentecost, Peter told the wondering observers, " 'Repent, and let every one of you be baptized in the name of Jesus Christ for the remission of sins; and you shall receive the gift of the Holy Spirit' " (Acts 2:38).

The word *repent* doesn't go over well in the twenty-first century because it implies responsibility. There's a mind-set that thinks that everything wrong is the fault of someone else, usually the parents. The present generation could very well be the one referred to in Proverbs: "There is a generation that curses its father, / And does not bless its mother. / There is a generation that is pure in its own eyes, / Yet is not washed from its filthiness" (Proverbs 30:11, 12).

The generation spoken of seems to think that anything and everything and anyone and everyone but themselves is responsible for what they've done and what they're doing. While there can be no doubt that many come from seriously dysfunctional families, the call to repent implies that what people are today is what they have chosen to be, because there were other options.

The call to repent is a call to a new beginning. Repentance is what grace uses to heal the wounds sin has inflicted on us, whether sins committed against us or sins that we've committed. One of the most wonderful promises in all of Scripture is the one that says, "If we confess our sins, He is faithful and just to forgive us our sins and to cleanse us from all unrighteousness" (1 John 1:9).

A NEW LIFE

A life that manifests the fruit of the Spirit is a new life, and there can be no new life while the old life remains. Remember the old saying that you can't make a silk purse out of a sow's ear. "Do you not know that the unrighteous will not inherit the kingdom of God? Do not be deceived. Neither fornicators, nor idolaters, nor adulterers, nor homosexuals, nor sodomites, nor thieves, nor covetous, nor drunkards, nor revilers, nor extortioners will inherit the kingdom of God" (1 Corinthians 6:9, 10). That's a strong warning—but notice the verse that follows: "And such *were* some of you. But you were washed, but you were sanctified, but you were justified in the name of the Lord Jesus and by the Spirit of our God" (verse 11; emphasis added).

One night during testimony time in a revival service I was conducting, a man stood up and said, "I used to be an alcoholic but Jesus has set me free." Paul's testimony is true: "And such *were* some of you."

Jesus told Nicodemus that he had to be born again (John 3:3). How does this work? It's truly as much a miracle as life itself. When we were born of our mothers, we began to live. When Jesus talked about being born again, He meant that we should leave the past behind and begin a new life. "If anyone is in Christ, he is a new creation; old things have passed away; behold, all things have become new" (2 Corinthians 5:17).

You've read the story before. It's found in Matthew 6:25–34. The disciples must have been expressing concerns for the kinds of things that concern us today, because Jesus told them not to worry about where their next meal was coming from or if they were going to be able to buy the clothes they needed. He reminded them that God provides for the plants and the animals that He made. "So don't worry," Jesus said. "Your heavenly Father knows what you need."

Jesus' counsel—no, it was a command—was that the disciples must not place their emphasis on obtaining food and clothes. Not that these things are unimportant, but it's a matter of putting first things first. Seek first the kingdom of God and His righteousness, and everything else will fall into place (Matthew 6:33).

The disciples might have asked among themselves, "What does He mean by saying that we're to seek first the kingdom of God? What's the kingdom of God?"

Romans 14:17 answers that question. It says, "The kingdom of God is not eating and drinking, but righteousness and peace and joy in the Holy Spirit."

When we read these texts, we become aware that we tend to be concerned with exactly what Jesus told us not to worry about. The point Jesus makes when He says to seek first the kingdom of God is that the most important thing in our lives should be to stay connected to Jesus, who is the Vine. Then we'll produce the fruit of the Spirit—the evidence of that connection.

Earlier, we learned that the fruit of the Spirit becomes most apparent when times are hardest. This means that when we put first things first, we will know by experience the meaning of the text that says, "All things work together for good to those who love God, to those who are the called according to His purpose" (Romans 8:28). Seeking first the fruit of the Spirit, then, is a win-win situation, because no matter what happens to us, we continue to grow.

It's called the fruit of the Spirit because it's the Holy Spirit who plants the seeds of the fruit in our hearts. We can't make the seeds germinate, but we can either encourage their growth or kill them. We have to deliberately kill the plant, because plants naturally strive to grow. That's the way God made them.

Speaking of encouraging the fruit of the Spirit to grow, I feel I must touch on an important, albeit sensitive area. A book on fruit cultivation would do an injustice if it didn't point out some of the worst pests that could destroy the fruit. It's probably a good thing that I saved this for the last chapter. I've found that the television programs many Christians watch nurture exactly the opposite of everything the Holy Spirit is trying to do in our lives. There's nothing that affects the growth of the fruit of the Spirit in our lives as does television. If the Lord has used this medium to save thousands, the devil has also used it to kill tens of thousands. I don't believe we need to write a PhD thesis to document the effect that television has on our culture, our church, our homes, and our personal spiritual lives.

If saturating ourselves in simulated sex, lying, stealing, murder, and all the rest doesn't destroy the fruit of the Spirit altogether, it will at least result in our becoming as "a sounding brass or a clanging cymbal" (1 Corinthians 13:1) or, put another way, "having a form of godliness but denying its power" (2 Timothy 3:5). The fruit of the Spirit will not grow in an environment that is so obviously contrary to the principles for which it was given.

WE CAN'T HAVE IT BOTH WAYS

On one of my preaching trips, my host had taken me back to the motel room for the night. I didn't have anything to do for an hour or two, so I decided to watch TV. I didn't watch HBO or dirty movies, just the regular programming of a local channel. When it came time to climb into bed, I knelt down and began to pray.

Of course, I always pray that I will be like Jesus. This time, though, after I said those words, I stopped where I was and decided that my prayer was not only ridiculous, it was insulting. Here I was, praying that I might have the Holy Spirit in my life, when for the last several hours I had been watching programs that were inconsistent with what I was asking Him to do in my life. How could Jesus answer my prayer?

I realized that night that I couldn't have it both ways. What was I going to do with the text that says, "Do not love the world or the things in the world. If anyone loves the world, the love of the Father is not in him" (1 John 2:15)? And even more to the point was the text: "Do you not know that friendship with the world is enmity with God?

Whoever therefore wants to be a friend of the world makes himself an enemy of God" (James 4:4). Then there's what Paul wrote: "Whatever things are true, whatever things are noble, whatever things are just, whatever things are pure, whatever things are lovely, whatever things are of good report, if there is any virtue and if there is anything praiseworthy—meditate on these things" (Philippians 4:8).

Dear reader, if we lay the TV programs that are usually watched alongside the fruit of the Spirit, we'll see that something has got to go. The text "Do not be unequally yoked together with unbelievers. For what fellowship has righteousness with lawlessness? And what communion has light with darkness?" (2 Corinthians 6:14) isn't referring just to whom we should marry. It's guidance meant for many parts of our lives.

To teach eternal truth, Jesus told stories from real life. One of these is the parable of the sower (Mark 4:3–20). In those days, seed was not drilled into the ground by large machines. First, the ground was plowed, and next the seeds were broadcast—that is, scattered by hand on top of the ground. Then the area that had been sown would be raked so that soil covered the seeds. It's not surprising that when the seed was broadcast, some of it would fall on the path that ran alongside the field. Some seed would fall along the sides of the field where the soil had not been prepared and the stones hadn't been removed. Some would fall on places that hadn't been planted the previous year and so had become weedy. But most of the seed would fall on the good ground, and it was from there that the harvest would come.

I don't claim to be a farmer, but I do have two eight-by-eight grow boxes in my backyard. I grow onions, lettuce, cabbage, and other kitchen vegetables. I grow them in the winter months because the summer is too hot and humid for these kinds of crops. Weeds are a problem in grow boxes as well as in flower beds and big fields. If you've grown flowers and vegetables, you've noticed that weeds grow easily and require little care!

To grow the fruit of the Spirit well, the weeds must be continually controlled. Like thorns and thistles, some weeds of the spiritual life may be easy to recognize. However, others may be like dandelions that look like pretty yellow flowers, yet can take over a lawn. Like weeds, the cares of this life that choke out the fruit of the Spirit are all the things that keep us from giving priority to the kingdom of God and His righteousness.

Like any garden, the spiritual life has two challenges. One is to fight the weeds, and the other is to nurture the fruit. We nurture the fruit of the Spirit through our devotional life. That's what keeps the fruit of the Spirit alive and well. Through prayer, we communicate with God, and through His Word, He communicates with us. Without the devotional life, the fruit of the Spirit becomes stunted, and then the cares of this life may simply choke it out.

AN ALTAR CALL

We've come to the end of this chapter and of this book. I'm going to close with an altar call. It is, of course, not an altar call in a church, but you may want to go to a place where you can be alone with God as you read the next few paragraphs.

I invite you first, with me, to thank God for His inestimable Gift, Jesus. In the olden days, going down to the altar was about repenting and being born again. Repentance and rebirth aren't things we do just once in a lifetime. We must experience them every day.

My appeal to you is that you look into your heart and see if thorns and thistles are choking out what Jesus wants to do for you. Look into your life and make sure that you are really born again—that is, that you are not carrying baggage from the past. The purpose of the gospel is to give us a new start. And after you have examined your condition, won't you join me in asking God to send the Holy Spirit to remind us to put first things first and to continually, every day, be growing the fruit of the Spirit in our lives?

Our first mission field is our homes, and unfortunately, that's the hardest place to be a Christian. The enemy is trying to destroy our homes. But when the devil comes in like a flood, the promise is that God will raise up a standard against him. That standard is the perfect life of Jesus, which in our lives is the fruit of the Spirit.

The enemy continues to try to divide and bring confusion. The fruit of the Spirit in our lives will put out the fires of dissent in our homes and in the church. It's what we are—through the Holy Spirit—that counts.

"Now may the God of peace who brought up our Lord Jesus from the dead, that great Shepherd of the sheep, through the blood of the everlasting covenant, make you complete in every good work to do His will, working in you in His sight, through Jesus Christ, to whom be glory forever and ever. Amen" (Hebrews 13:20, 21).